NO PLACE
FOR FOP OR IDLER

Here's no place for fop or idler; they who made our city great
Feared no hardship, shirked no labour, smiled at death and conquered fate;
They who gave our school its laurels laid on us a sacred trust;
Forward therefore, live your hardest, die of service, not of rust.

From *King Edward's School Song.*
by Alfred Hayes, OE

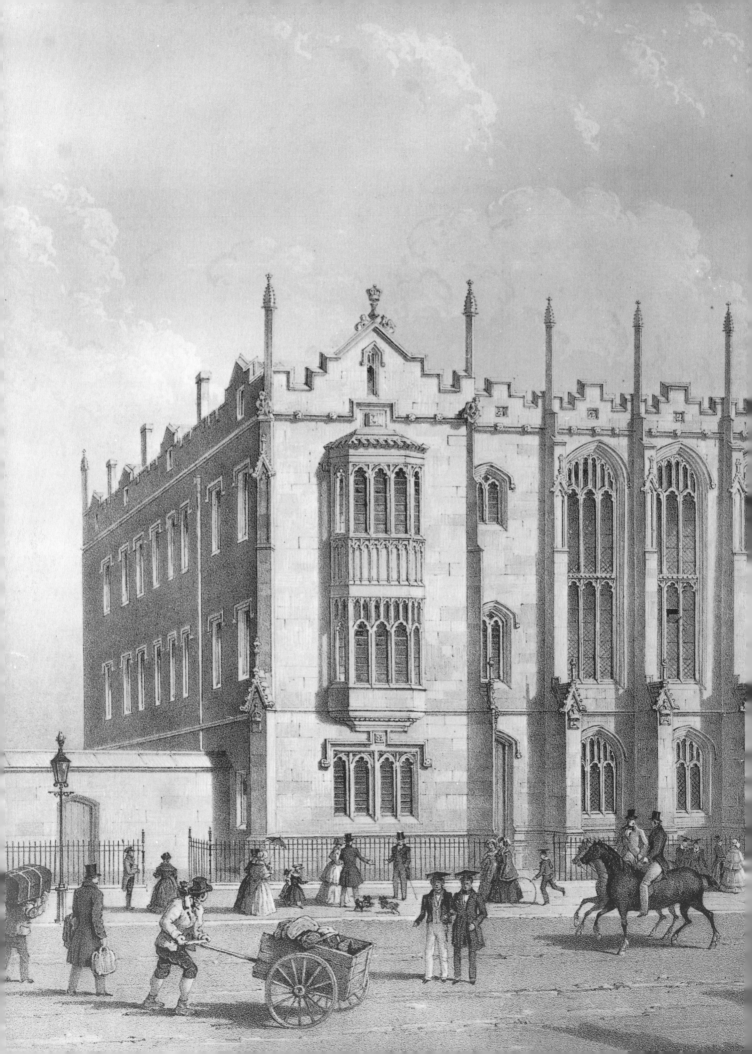

NO PLACE FOR FOP OR IDLER

The Story of King Edward's School, Birmingham

ANTHONY TROTT

EDGBASTON & BIRMINGHAM

JAMES X JAMES

To all the Assistant Masters
past and present
of King Edward's School,
Birmingham

The publishers are grateful to the following for
permission to reproduce illustrations:
National Portrait Gallery (pp. 20, 27, 31 and
Colour Plate 1); The City Museum and Art Gallery,
Birmingham (p. 51 and Colour Plates 4 & 5);
Mary Evans Picture Library (pp. 21, 43, 47);
and also to Faber & Faber Ltd.
for permission to quote
from T.S. Eliot's *The Cocktail Party*
on p. 104 and from W.H. Auden's
Collected Shorter Poems on p. 126

First published 1992

ISBN 0 907383 31 9

Designed by Tom Cabot

Typeset by Action Typesetting, Gloucester
Printed in the Great Britain by
Hollen Street Press Limited, Berkshire
Published by James and James (Publishers) Limited
75 Carleton Road,
London N7 0ET

Half-title page: The Georgian school building in
New Street.

Title page: Barry's building in New Street, from a
mid-nineteenth century engraving.

Contents

Foreword

THE REPUTATION of King Edward's School has never been higher than it is now. This, combined with the celebration of the 600th anniversary of the foundation of the Guild of the Holy Cross in July 1392, from which the modern foundation stems, provide an excellent reason for a further examination of the origins and development of this famous school. The programme of expansion of the school in recent years, now all but complete, also provides a reason for a backwards look to see how the school's expansion in the past has affected it, both by looking inwards at the varied activities of the School and the personalities of those in it, and also by looking outwards at its relations with the City of Birmingham and its position in the national educational scene. Much of value can be learned.

The debt that any historian of the School owes to T.W. Hutton, whose history was published by Basil Blackwell in 1952, is obvious, but each generation has the task of re-interpreting the past and bringing history up to date. Tony Trott has an extremely long acquaintance with the school and a deep love for it, having served on the staff for nearly 40 years, for most of this time as Head of English. He is to be congratulated, therefore, not only on the timing of his History, but also on the real insight that his own personal recollections and his re-examination of the sources provide into the nature and history of a school that, as well as being famous, is held in such high regard not only nationally but also by its parents, pupils and Old Boys.

Chairman of Governors

Chief Master,
King Edward's School.

I am delighted to welcome this fine new history of the school. I strongly commend it to Edwardians of all ages and indeed to everyone with an interest in education. As we approach the twenty-first century there could be no more timely reminder that in a time of rapid and radical change an appreciation of our history can serve us well.

Bailiff

Preface

THE STORY OF a school may be written from any one of several points of view, each of which will exhibit its own partialities. As the dedication of this book will have made clear this is unashamedly a master's tale and it is none the worse for that. After all, it is masters, good, bad and indifferent, who bulk large in men's memories of their time in school; and when one thinks of those whose whole career has been devoted to the service of a school – in the case of King Edward's School, Greene in the eighteenth century, Rann Kennedy and Gedge in the early nineteenth century, Levett and Hunter Smith in the later nineteenth century, Heath, Acatos, Langley, Roberts, Craig, Biggs and several others in the present century – it is masters who provide the essential continuity of a school's life. They have some claim to speak for it.

I can make no claim to fundamental research. This has been done some time since and is digested in two indispensable books, T. W. Hutton's *King Edward's School, Birmingham 1552–1952* (1952) and Carl Boardman's *Foundation and City* (1985). Hutton's book was written *con amore* by an Old Edwardian who became a school governor. It is full of detail about almost every aspect of school life but is inclined to be over-reverential towards its subject and suffers from seeing the school in a historical vacuum rather than bedded in the life of its time. This deficiency is more than compensated in Boardman's vastly informative study of the King Edward's Foundation. His book was the result of five years' work in the school archives and it is a matter of astonishment and regret that no commercial publisher could be found for it. It was left to the governors of the school to issue a small private imprint of this invaluable book to which I am greatly indebted at many points in the first four chapters of the present history.

Considerations of space have compelled to me to omit much that I would have liked to include – details of the feuds between governors and subsequent legal battles that occurred in the late sixteenth and throughout the seventeenth century, an account of the Milward Foundation in the seventeenth century and of the Hill Benefaction in the eighteenth century. I am conscious of an imbalance in the list of old boys that follows the main narrative. It does not do justice to the large numbers of first-class scientists that the school has produced since the Second World War. I am sorry about this but can only write from the information that I have been able to obtain and must echo Dr Johnson's reply when challenged to account for an error in his *Dictionary* – 'Ignorance, madam'.

I am very grateful to all OEs who have helped me with photographs, information and opinions. Anecdotes that I have not been able to find room for have, nevertheless, been as useful in helping me to form a view of the subject under discussion as those that I have used. I am particularly indebted to two former colleagues, Norman Craig and Tom Freeman, OEs both, who have been enormously helpful in enabling me to build up a picture of the school between the wars. I am grateful, too, to the new Chief Master, Hugh Wright, for reading this book and for giving me valuable assistance in the tricky business of identifying for excision those passages which would strike the candid reader as not strictly necessary. I should like also to thank three former Chief Masters, Ronald Lunt, Robson Fisher and Martin Rogers for their reflections on their respective Chief Masterships. I must additionally thank Martin Rogers for the invitation to write this book and Ronald Lunt for much miscellaneous information, for the meticulous and vigilant care with which he read my typescript and, above all, for hearteningly enthusiastic encouragement.

Finally, I must thank my wife and my publisher, Mr Hamish MacGibbon, for a great deal of help and support, and Mrs Anne Baird for her fine colour photographs of paintings in the school.

John Rogers was the first of the Protestant martyrs to be burned in the reign of Queen Mary. He was a Birmingham man and went to the school of the Guild of St John the Baptist which was suppressed by the act of Parliament which ironically led to the foundation of King Edward's school (see page 11).

1

In the Beginning

He (Dr Johnson) was reading. I asked what book he had got. He said the
History of Birmingham. Local histories, I observed, were generally dull. 'It
is true, sir; but this has a peculiar merit with me; for I passed some of my
early years and married my wife there.'

Sir James Prior: *Life of Edmund Malone*

It would be gratifying to be able to claim that the foundation of a 'free
grammar school' in Birmingham in 1552 was an act of unalloyed, educational
idealism. But, alas, there was little in the life of mid-sixteenth-century England
that was unalloyed; we have not for some time been able to share that innocent
Protestant conviction which saw the reign of 'our pious founder and benefactor,
King Edward VI', as a time when it was bliss to be alive. England was far from
being a happy country; the times were too complex and uncertain. Indeed,
anyone under twenty in the year of the school's foundation would have lived his
whole life in an atmosphere of rapid and bewildering change. Because King
Edward's School came into being as a direct consequence of the public policy of
a radically reforming government it may be worth while to dwell briefly on some
features of the world into which it was born, a world where idealism could not
escape the taint of hard-headed opportunism and where most policy decisions
were morally ambiguous.

The Birmingham citizen of 1552 would have been well aware of the
multiplicity of facts which showed that 'the world, it is a-changin'. Consider
the following. Enclosures, unemployment and inflation were evidence of
economic instability that bore heavily on large sections of the community, and
when the government imposed price controls it merely drew attention to the fact
that all was not well with the economy. Two significant rebellions had taken
place within the previous twenty years and both had been suppressed by the
king's generals with considerable ferocity. A self-willed, capricious and ruthless
king had been succeeded by a boy-king, and boy-kings raised alarming memories.
Within the same period the old king had had no fewer than six queens, two of

whom he had divorced and two executed. He had also extended the treason laws to include more possibilities than ever before (or since). But more disruptive than anything else he had set about transforming and partially dismantling the nation's most ancient institution, the Church. Whatever its undoubted shortcomings the traditional Church was organically entwined in the emotional and social patterns of men's lives, more deeply rooted than either parliament or the monarchy. To see, in the space of a few years, the Church detached from its leadership in Rome, its monastic institutions suppressed, its liturgy remodelled and some of its distinguished figures barbarously executed constituted an act of violence to the psychic and emotional life of the nation. Yet it was this same determination to refashion the Church that caused the foundation of King Edward's School.

The Act which set in motion the process that led to the establishment of the school was passed by the House of Commons just before Christmas in 1547. It was a law whereby 'certain chantries, colleges, free chapels and the possessions of the same be given to the king's majesty'. Contrary to what is sometimes thought a chantry was not a building but an endowment or benefaction, partly charitable, partly self-interested, to be used for religious and social purposes. In 1382 four Birmingham citizens had petitioned Richard II for a licence to endow two chantry priests in the church of St Martin in Birmingham and ten years later, in 1392, the letters patent had been issued to bring this about. The resulting Guild of the Holy Cross, with a total endowment of £7.13s.0d., was a society with mixed purposes: worship, charity to the sick and poor, civic works and mutual assistance. It did not, however, engage in education, as guilds often did when one of their stipendiary priests undertook a teaching responsibility. Indeed, a sister guild in Birmingham, the Guild of St John the Baptist at Deritend, fulfilled just such a function. It taught boys in its hall and it employed a schoolmaster.

In 1545 Henry VIII had appointed commissioners to inspect chantries and guilds and to confiscate the property of those that were not fulfilling the terms of the donors' bequests. But lest it be supposed that reformation alone was the king's motive it is well to remember that the statute itself made it clear that the immediate motive was the need to raise money for military action against Scotland and France. From this inquisition the two Birmingham guilds emerged untouched. In 1547, however, the commissioners of the new, young king were less accommodating and found that a very high proportion of the funds of the Guild of the Holy Cross was spent on religious rather than on charitable activities. The fate of the guild was sealed. So, apparently, was that of the Guild of St John the Baptist.

It was at this point that the Guild of the Holy Cross developed an interest in education. The Act of 1547 had suggested that where a guild or fraternity already kept a school it might retain the lands to support it. Although the Guild of the Holy Cross had never before concerned itself with education, in 1548 some Birmingham citizens, led by Richard Smalbroke, pushed their luck to petition the Crown for the return of the Guild's lands, not to continue a school but to start one. And the surprising fact is that they succeeded where their sister Guild of St John the Baptist, which already supported a school, failed.

Seal of the Guild of the Holy Cross.

Perhaps the fact is not as paradoxical as it may at first appear. To simplify an involved situation, the lord of the manor of Birmingham was John Dudley, Duke of Northumberland, at that time one of the most powerful men in England. Of all the hard-faced men who had done well out of the suppression of the monasteries he was probably the hardest. He was to gain control of the Council and bring about the fall of the Lord Protector Somerset, whom he sent to the block three weeks after the Birmingham school received its charter, and he was a widely unpopular figure. Not surprisingly, therefore, he was anxious to create support in the country and had been prepared to court the goodwill of Birmingham by, among other things, granting favourable leases to the town's most influential citizens. Many of these were likely to have been members of the Guild of the Holy Cross and it made sense to secure their support. Northumberland was riding high, and when he had eliminated his rival the Guild of the Holy Cross, against obvious expectations, received back for the purpose of founding a school a significant proportion of its property (which between 1392 and 1552 had appreciated in value from £7.13s.0d. to £32.12s.5d.). In spite of its existing school the Guild of St John the Baptist, which clearly lacked a voice in the places that mattered, sank without trace. A severe moralist might find the whole transaction slightly less than edifying.

The charter of 2 January 1552 declares that the king will grant and ordain that:

> from henceforth there is and shalbe one grammer Schoole in Birmingham aforeseyd whiche shalbe callid the free Grammer Schole of Kinge Edwarde the Sixte for the educacion and instruccion and institucion of children and younge men in Grammer forever to endure, And that same Schole of one schole master and one usher for ever to continewe we do erecte make ordeyne and establishe by these presents, And for that our seyd entente maye take the more effecte, and that the lands Tenements Rents Revenues and other thinges to be given assigned and appointed for the mayntenance of the seyd Schole maye be the better gouerned for the continuance of the seyd Schoole we will and ordeyne that from hencefourth there be and shalbe twentie honeste and discrete men Inhabitants of the towne and parishe of Birmingham or of the lordshippe to the seyd towne adioyninge in the seyd countie of Warwick for the tyme being, whche be and shalbe callid Gouernors of the possessions Revenewes and goods of the seyd Schoole comonly callid and to be callid the free grammer Schoole of Kinge Edwarde the Sixte in Birmingham in the countie of Warwick.

Although the commission of 1547 had limited the amount of returnable property to the value of £20 per annum the town, in fact, received £21 to take account of the annual £1 payable to the Crown as rent. It will be noted that the twenty 'honeste and discrete men' who were to constitute the corporate body of 'Governours of the possessions, Revenewes and goods of the seyd Schoole' were to be 'Inhabitants of the towne and parishe of Birmingham or of the lordshippe of Birmingham to the seyd towne adioyninge'. It is clear that the first governing body was drawn to a considerable extent from the great and good of Birmingham itself, the families of Colmore and Smalbroke being the most prominent; and because Birmingham as a town had no charter of incorporation which would have enabled its citizens to speak legally with a collective voice the governing body of the 'free grammer school' was able to offer the next best thing and naturally attracted to itself the influential élite of the town. Moreover, it looked likely to stay that way because the governors were elected for life and among their considerable powers was that of electing, in the event of one of them dying, a replacement to their own number without outside interference.

One may wonder whether, as trustees of extensive property and representatives of the expanding energy of the town, educational interests were always at the top of their agenda. Naturally, the governors sent their own sons to the school and equally naturally it was often the governors' personal connections that shaped the school's affairs. For instance, Mary, one of the powerful Colmore clan, married some time before 1591 Dr Richard Harris, Principal of Brasenose College, Oxford, and this seems to have cemented what was already a regular connection between the school and the college. This was not always to the school's advantage, for in 1598 they appointed, on the advice of 'seventeen learned men' of the college, Richard Billingsley, bursar of the college and an old boy of the school, to the post of pedagogue, a post he continued to hold for nearly forty years but with notable lack of distinction. And Thomas Colmore, who became an MA and Fellow of the College in 1583, was expelled therefrom ten years later because seven years after proceeding to his master's degree he had not entered holy orders ('quod infra septem annos postquam susceperat gradum magistrum sacros ordines non habuerat et Presbyter non fuerat').

Apart from the possession of a common seal, symbol of collective authority, the governors had the power to appoint the master and the usher and to frame:

> fit and wholesome Statutes and Ordinances ... concerning and touching the Order, Government and Direction of the Pedagogue and Sub-Pedagogue and Scholars of the aforesaid School for the time being, and of the Stipend and Salary of the said Pedagogue and Sub-Pedagogue.

The governors' primary function was to administer a trust and to 'establish and maintain a school'. Income was to be used to employ a *pedagogus* (master) and a *subpedagogus* (usher) and for nothing else, a concept which in the context of present-day practice would appear eccentric to the point of perversity. No mention is made of buildings. Two further observations may be made. The phrase 'free grammar school' meant what it appears to mean, that the pupils did not have to pay for their education. The phrase is a common one in sixteenth-century educational charters but, in the past, attempts have been made by other schools to suggest that 'free' means free from external, i.e. ecclesiastical, jurisdiction. This interpretation was demolished in 1908 by the great educational historian, A. F. Leach. His arguments were simple, based upon the usage of the word 'libera' and on medieval and sixteenth-century history, but the evidence that Leach produced in support of them is pulverising. The second observation is that the charter is not specific about the catchment area of those pupils who qualify for free education, whether it should be limited to the town or the manor or not at all. The overall position is summed up by T. W. Hutton:

> The points specially to be noted are the composition of the governing body, its independence and its capacity for self-perpetuation; the narrow scope laid down for the activities of the charity; and the difficulties of change even when change was both desirable and desired.

To make sure that the school operated as an arm of the new order in which the sovereign was not only head of State but head of the Church as well, master of both the bodies and the souls of his people, statutes devised by the governors were to be framed with the advice of the diocesan bishop.

What did the first generation of pupils in this new school learn? We all know that Latin and, to a lesser extent, Greek constituted the entire curriculum of sixteenth-century grammar schools. 'Grammar' meant Latin grammar. But upon this common base and upon a corpus of Latin texts that was common to all European schools refinements of detail were superimposed. Renaissance humanists were never slow to give advice on almost any topic and, not surprisingly, education was a favourite one. Each individual sage propounded his preferred syllabus. Such great figures as Erasmus and, even more, Vives, had each spent quite some time in England and were well known to English contemporaries, and both had much to say about how Latin should be taught and what its value was. Both were closely connected with educationists such as Colet and Lily and all of them had produced practical Latin courses. But bearing in mind the date and the circumstances of King Edward's School's foundation what one would like to know is whether the teaching primers of Erasmus and Vives were replaced by those of Castellion and Cordier which evinced a decidedly Protestant orientation and which were being used in England in the second half of the century.

Latin was essential to the process of 'getting on'. Its relevance to a career in the Church or the law is obvious, but no less important was its relevance to almost any kind of career in administration or government, largely because some knowledge of the law was an essential requirement for such a career. For all who hoped to rise in the world Latin was a *sine qua non*. This was not because it was held to provide uniquely effective circuit training for the mind – a view that has had its impassioned advocates among educationists in more recent times – but because it was the language in which a great part of the wisdom of Western civilisation was expressed. It was thus through Latin texts that a knowledge of the course of human affairs was acquired and of natural history too; Pliny the Elder was among the authors commonly read. Moreover, Latin was held to be the seed-bed of eloquence and it was a combination of knowledge and eloquence that fitted men to be 'profitable members of the Church and Commonwealth'. To a lesser extent the same was held to be true of Greek, but as there were fewer competent teachers of Greek it was in practice Latin that dominated school curricula. Where Greek was taught its value was felt to be not so much in Homer and the Greek dramatists (who were hardly known), or even in the philosophers, as in the fact that knowledge of Greek enabled the student to get closer to the meaning of the New Testament. The value of knowing classical languages, although rooted in their content, had little to do with sweetness and light; it was unashamedly utilitarian.

It may seem at first that this specialised education was hardly suitable for the sons of the citizens of Birmingham, a large village that, in 1552, was in the process of becoming a small town, where trade, manufacture and agriculture were inextricably enmeshed. By the end of the century it was no longer

13

Part of the Manor of Birmingham in 1553. The building marked 'Gild Hall' in New Street was the site of the school from its foundation until 1935.

principally a town of tanners, fullers and wool manufacturers. The smiths, who had been noted by Leland in his *Itinerary* (1538), had taken over; by 1600, iron and steel goods were the dominant local products. In the year of the school's foundation Gill* tells us that in an estimated population of about 1500:

> There were probably 300 labourers, journeymen and apprentices, who paid no direct taxes. Above them was a class of small craftsmen, yeomen and the like, about 120 in number who were liable to pay poll-taxes, but were exempt from taxes on property. The bulk of the population belonged to these two classes. There were in Birmingham between sixty and seventy 'subsidy men', manufacturers, shopkeepers and merchants who were assessed on their property; and among them a dozen or more members of well-to-do families formed a local aristocracy [not to be confused with the local gentry].

Though the education offered at King Edward's School was free to all the cost to poor families would have been serious because it would have meant a reduction in the family earning-power over a period of years. The endowment made no provision for scholarships. It is doubtful if the 420 families in Gill's first two

* Conrad Gill, *History of Birmingham (vol. i)*, OUP, 1952.

categories could have afforded this. Moreover, the education offered was not directly relevant to their needs as its logical termination was the university and, as Roger Ascham wrote to Archbishop Cranmer in 1547, the students being admitted to Cambridge were 'for the most part only the sons of rich men and such as never intended to pursue their studies to that degree as to arrive at an eminent proficiency and perfection of learning but only to qualify themselves for some place in the state'.

One must suppose, therefore, that it was probably from the families of the 70-odd 'subsidy men', Gill's third category, that most of the first generation pupils of King Edward's School were drawn. If this supposition is right it tightens the link between the school and the town élite, for it was their sons whose putative career aspirations would most likely have benefited from a grammar school education. An example is conveniently to hand in the career of Clement Colmore, brother of the Thomas Colmore who was expelled from Brasenose College in 1593. He left the school in 1566, matriculated at Brasenose College, Oxford, became a Fellow of the college, a proctor in the university, Chancellor of Durham, and one of Elizabeth's commissioners to treat with the Scots in 1596. Perhaps he was one of the 'great learned men who have had their instruction and education' at King Edward's School who were later to be mentioned in the Bill of Complaint brought by seventeen governors against one other and his accomplice in 1604. If not exactly a 'great learned man' Richard Shilton became Solicitor-General under Charles I and was knighted before becoming, according to Clarendon, 'an old, illiterate, useless person'. Both men, along with at least nine others who adorned the law or the Church or the governing body, had passed through the universities before the turn of the century.

One further development occurred during the first fifty years of the school's existence that should be noted. In 1596 the governors issued Statutes and Ordinances as required by the original charter. They were stringent and restrictive and aimed at clarifying the position of their tenants and keeping their teachers on a distinctly tight rein. What is slightly offensive about them is the minatory tone rather than the substance of what is said. The schoolmaster must accept whatever salary was offered 'without finding himself grieved or complaining, except to the Governors'. (It must in fairness be said that between 1552 and 1598 the schoolmaster's salary rose from £6.13s.4d. to £20 per annum and the usher's from £2 to £10 per annum.) He must never criticise the governors or the founding charter, he must secure permission for any absence and he 'must obey and observe all such orders as the Governors should from time to tyme thereafter make prescribe or ordeine for the disposeing or governing of the schoole and revenue thereof the schoolmaster usher or schollers or any of them'. One detects a touch of power-mania in the almost hysterical crescendo of that final sentence. It is perhaps little wonder that Bishop Overton did not confirm these ordinances despite the *douceur* of wine and sugar-loaf that he was offered.

2

Legal Proceedings

'Soldiers finde warres, and Lawyers finde out still
Litigious men, which quarrels move . . .'

John Donne: *The Canonization*

IN 1604 A SUIT was begun in Chancery by seventeen governors of King
Edward's School against Thomas Smalbroke and Ambrose Colmore. It was the
product of faction fighting which, in its turn, was the product of a power
struggle between their respective families, two of the most influential among the
oligarchs of Birmingham and both represented on the school's governing body.*
The reader who is familiar with Icelandic sagas or is an *aficionado* of the classic
Hollywood Western will instantly feel at home among the sixteenth-century
governors of King Edward's School. Nor should this surprise us for there is a
common factor between life in Laxriverdale and Dodge City and Elizabethan
Warwickshire; in each case we encounter a world where small but dynamic
communities exhibit similar tensions between naked self-assertion and law.

However, while the governors quarrelled the school presumably went on with
its job under a succession of masters. It may be worth observing that the early
foundation documents refer to the master in charge of the school in various ways,
as 'pedagogue', as 'chief schoolmaster', as 'master', as 'schoolmaster'. Nearly
three centuries later, in 1883, he was to be designated 'headmaster' and later still,
in January 1953, it was decreed that he should be called 'Chief Master',
presumably because such a nomenclature had an archaic and therefore
distinguished ring to it. In the interest of consistency the pedagogues of King
Edward's School will henceforward be referred to in this narrative as Chief
Master as the term, though somewhat artificially created, has now been current
for nearly forty years.

The Chief Masters of the school's early years remain shadowy figures. Though
we do not know the exact length of time during which each held office,

* See Appendix 1.

16

PLATE 1   This interesting picture, painted by an unknown hand, shows the dying
Henry VIII handing on the gift of an independent Church of England to his son,
Edward. The row of patriarchally hairy figures (back right) includes the Duke of
Northumberland (first seated figure to the right of Edward). Some of the wicked
papists at the bottom of the picture are given the sort of faces usually reserved for the
damned in representations of the Day of Judgement.

PLATE 2 Copy by Mrs Verena Vickers of a portrait of Edward VI of which the
original hangs in the National Portrait Gallery.

T. W. Hutton gives the following approximate dates: Thomas Buther (1561?–1583?); William Woodwall (1583–1599); Richard Billingsley (1599–1637). Of Buther all that is certain is the date of his marriage in St Martin's Church register in 1561, where he is described as *Pedagogus Schol. Lib.* It is characteristic of the nature of the Foundation in the first century of its existence that he married into the Smalbroke family. His successor, William Woodwall, was the author of a work of the kind in which the age delighted called *The Acts of Queen Elizabeth Allegorised.* He in his turn was followed by Richard Billingsley who was to remain in office for nearly forty years and was prominent in the next major event to be described, another legal battle.

On 30 September 1633 a certain Mr Nicols sent a letter to Charles I's Secretary of State which drew attention to the fact that the lands given by previous sovereigns for the founding and maintenance of 'schools, hospitals, highways, bridges and the like' had appreciated considerably in value since they were granted and the revenues from them were now being misapplied. One instance only was given of this general proposition, that of 'the free school of the town of Birmingham'. This circumstance, plus the fact that nothing is known of Mr Nicols, makes it look as if someone was after King Edward's School and its governors. Mr Nicols's letter drew attention to the fact that the lands given to the school in 1552 and then valued at £20 per annum were now worth ten times that amount, that a great deal of timber from the lands had been sold and that the masters were being paid only £20 each per annum. (One may remember that the original charter stated that all revenues should be used for the 'sustenation' of the pedagogue and sub-pedagogue.) Nicols proposed that the king should 'take the managing of the revenues into his own hands'. The result of this seductive proposal would be that it would 'bring in to the king great profit in the present, and daily increase thereof for His Majesty and his successors by the future surplusages of the general great revenue'.

Mr Nicols's effort as a self-appointed director of policy studies to the king drew no immediate response from the government but by 1638 things had changed. Charles was finding resistance to his other methods of raising money and Birmingham was being seen, in Clarendon's words, as 'a town generally wicked . . . declaring a more peremptory malice to His Majesty than any other place'. So in that year the Attorney-General, Sir John Bankes, displayed a Bill of Information to the Lord Treasurer and the Barons of the Exchequer. This bill levels several weighty charges against the governors of King Edward's School. They are said to have manipulated leases and rents out of 'a greedy and covetous desire to enrich themselves' and 'to the utter disherison and destruction of the said school'. They had received an income of £545 per annum, vastly in excess of what was envisaged in the original assessment in 1552, and yet they were still only paying £20 per annum to each of the masters. This had compelled the masters to charge sixpence per week to children who should be taught free. They had elected 'unfit persons' to the governing body and had appointed 'unfit persons' to teach, as a result of which no boys had been sufficiently prepared for university entrance for forty years and parents had been forced to send their boys elsewhere. They had not consulted the bishop about 'making fit and wholesome statutes' and they had imposed on oath of secrecy on the Chief Master that he should not 'come against them and discover these their practices'. It looks as if there was a good deal of local feeling as well as knowledge behind these charges. The governors of King Edward's School appear not to have been universally loved in the neighbourhood.

They defended themselves against the charges in the Bill in a vigorous written reply of 12 October 1638. Much of their defence was a straight denial of the accuracy of the facts on which the charges were based. With the exception of one governor, Robert Shilton, they denied that they had sold off timber from Foundation properties except for that from old and decayed trees. (The sale of timber had been expressly prohibited in the leases, but the growth of the local iron industry and the consequent need of charcoal for smelting meant that there was always a demand for timber and that must have constituted a permanent temptation.) But there was real confusion over the matter of endowment income and the granting of leases. As long ago as 1565 most of the leases had been called in and regranted for ninety-nine years at low rents. The inflation that had occurred between 1565 and 1638 meant that a low but reasonable rent in 1565 was now quite unrealistic. As many of the leaseholders from 1565 had been governors or their relatives it was their families who were benefiting from the

Sir John Bankes. As Attorney-General for Charles I he presented the Bill of Information brought against the governors of the school in 1638.

18

situation rather than the Foundation as a whole, the property of which should have been generating a much higher income. At the same time leases that had not been surrendered and regranted in 1565 ran their natural course and when they fell in new leases carried higher rents in line with current land and property values. Looked at in one way the foundation was not realising its economic potential, and looked at in another some tenants appeared to be being milked. It would have seemed that there was inequity over rent levels, some would have said corruption. Yet the governors had not transgressed the Charter in any way, had not actually done anything legally wrong. Such was the muddled situation that was eventually argued before the Court of Exchequer in December 1638.

In their written reply that preceded that hearing the governors admitted the masters' low salary but pointed out that each of them enjoyed a house and garden rent-free. They denied that town boys had ever been charged and named three boys from the school, William Ailesbury, John Shilton and Henry Porter who had, in fact, proceeded to Oxford or Cambridge within the previous twelve years. (Actually Henry Porter's name does not appear in the *Alumnni Cantab.* but William Harrison, a boy not named by the governors, was at the time of their reply about to go to Oxford. He went up to Christ Church in 1639 while the case was still rumbling on.) The governors claimed that the Chief Master, Mr Billingsley, had been recommended by 'seventeen learned men of Brazen Nose College in Oxford' and that on his appointment he had taken no oath of secrecy. As Mr Billingsley had been Chief Master for thirty-nine years (since 1599) there was only one governor who had served long enough to remember the facts. He was the indestructible Luke Smyth, Rector of St Martin's since 1578, a living to which he had been presented by his father who had been one of the original 1552 governors of the school. At the age of eighty-four he spoke with the authority of Nestor. With the work of the Usher, Mr Grundy, the governors professed themselves well-satisfied; all spoke well of him. A final point made in the governors' defence is worth noting, the claim that the reason why more boys had not proceeded to the universities was that their parents 'would have their children brought up for trades rather than be at the charges in maintaining them in the universities'. The 'city of a thousand trades' was in the making.

The Crown was not impressed by the governors' answers which they evidently did not believe and repeated their own charges. After the hearing no Order seems to have been made and later, in June 1639, the court learned that the school's tenants had agreed to double the rents. They seem not to have viewed the prospect of Charles I as landlord with much enthusiasm and had the case gone badly against the governors this could well have been the result. They said that they were making such an agreement so that the Chief Master and the Usher could be decently paid and they added, ominously, 'provided there be choice made of an able and sufficient man to be Schoolmaster'. So in 1640 Billingsley was demoted to Usher, a new Chief Master was appointed and the luckless Grundy (of whom everybody spoke well) being at the point where the buck stopped, carried the can into oblivion.

The result of this Bill brought against the governors of the free grammar school was inconclusive as with the outbreak of the Civil War in 1642 litigation came to an end. With respect to the great issues that convulsed the nation the stance of Birmingham was, on the whole, parliamentarian. The town was beginning the process of industrialisation that was to accelerate in the second half of the century, and men making a place for themselves in the world – the increasingly affluent and therefore influential ironmasters – did not automatically take their religious/political allegiances from the local landowning gentry. As the quotation from Clarendon (p. 17) suggests, Birmingham's allegiances were not calculated to please the royalist party. Indeed, there is a suspicion that the Bill of Complaint of 1638 may have had its inspiration in the feelings of Sir Thomas Holte of Aston Hall, the most influential local gentleman, a strong royalist who entertained Charles I for two nights a few days before the Battle of Edgehill. To such local gentry the governors of the free grammar school were a permanent reminder of an independent urban power which was out of their control. Moreover, the temper of the town was increasingly opposed to the king's religious policy. So when, in 1643, Prince Rupert led a raiding force north from Oxford to establish royal power in Lichfield the citizenry of Birmingham, albeit against the advice of the most influential among them, barred his way at Camp Hill and Digbeth. The result was a skirmish and the royal detachment occupied the town (against their commander's original intention), looted and burned property, much of it foundation property, and in the course of the fighting killed fourteen citizens. One of these was a school governor, John Carter, and four others were from families that were or had been on the governing body – Elsmore, Turton, Rastell and Billingsley.

After the royalist pillage of the town an anonymous pamphlet appeared entitled *Prince Rupert's Burning Love to England Discovered in the Flames of Birmingham*. A case has been made out that the author was John Barton who succeeded Billingsley as Chief Master of the Free Grammar School when the latter was demoted in 1639. The attribution of authorship remains speculative but suggestive arguments for it can be adduced. In the first place, the school had lost a good deal of property in the royal occupation; in the second, Barton was an associate of Francis Roberts, a resident minister of Birmingham of Puritan persuasion who had got out before Prince Rupert got in, and of Thomas Hall, the learned Puritan minister of neighbouring King's Norton; and in the third, the pamphlet's publisher was Thomas Underhill who also published another of Barton's books, *The Latine Grammar Composed in the English Tongue*. This latter book was published in 1652, some time after Barton left Birmingham in 1645. His successor, John Thompson, exists as little more than a name in the governors' accounts and it is at about this time that those accounts begin to register irregular payments to masters who are described as assistants, in addition to the Chief Master and Usher. In the year of the king's execution, 1649, the accounts record a change that was to bring to the school its first really commanding Chief Master. In that year Mr Thompson was paid £30 and a certain Mr Brokesby £10. As the annual salary for the Chief Master was £40 it looks as if Mr Brokesby took over about Michaelmas of that year. Although his appointment was not confirmed until 1654, he was paid a Chief Master's salary

Prince Rupert, Commander of royalist cavalry.

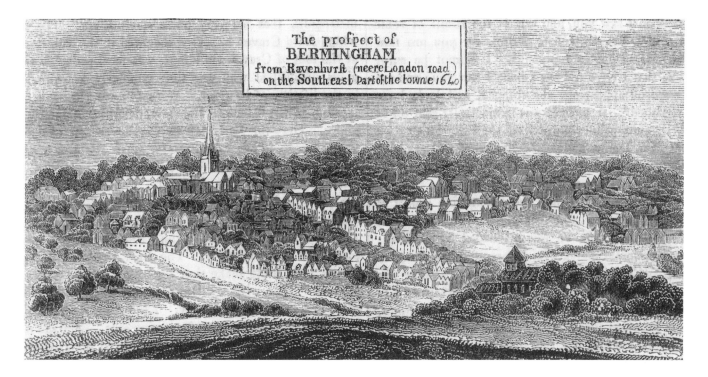

The prospect of
BERMINGHAM
from Ravenhurst (neere London road)
on the South east part of the towne 1640

Birmingham in 1620.

from the start and remained in the job for the next thirty-six years. He was the first Chief Master not to be in orders (and the only one until 1900) and to have proceeded only to a bachelor's degree and not a master's, a fact later to be used against him.

Brokesby had scarcely settled into the job when, in June 1650, he and seven of the fourteen governors were reported to the Committee of Indemnity for failing to take the engagement of loyalty to the Commonwealth. Those who failed to do so were barred by an Act of Parliament from any 'place of trust or profitt'. The petitioner who brought the matter to the notice of the Court, a Captain Robert Girdler, described the 'chief schoolmaster' as 'very much disaffected unto the State', and complained also that the governors were not paying their 'Under schoolmaster', Francis Reynolds, who was 'constantly well affected to the Parliament and present State'. This political storm in a teacup came to nothing as Brokesby and the recalcitrant governors rapidly conformed and Reynolds disappeared from sight. Girdler tried to push the case further, which makes it look as if personal animosities as well as political enthusiasm may have been involved, but he failed. Yet this incident suggests how facile it may be to apply conventional labels to people's attitudes at this time. Brokesby's alleged Puritanism does not seem to have been much in evidence here, and half of the governors of an independently-minded school in an independently-minded town had to be pushed into declaring for the New Order. It was a big jump, after all, from simply disliking the king's religious policies and keeping a wary distance from the landowning gentry to supporting a Commonwealth that had turned established order upside down by eliminating the monarch. However, politically moderate though the governors may in general have been they could not escape the all-absorbing conflict of religious ideologies, and as far as Birmingham was concerned that conflict often focused on the personality and doctrine of the incumbent of St Martin's. As he was often also a governor of the grammar school this connected the school with such disputes and they were sometimes violent. Moreover, the school's governors, being drawn largely from the controlling families of the town, were often employers or landlords, and working people came to see them as much an authoritarian establishment as the landowning gentry. So it is not surprising that eventually popular violence, schooled in religious confrontation, should erupt against the school itself.

The incident took place on 26 November 1667 and was the celebrated 'debarring'. Most schools with any pretension to pedigree can include in their annals scenes of picturesque violence offered by pupils to their masters. The particular interest of this incident is the readiness with which the town population exploited a fairly routine case of boys being unedifyingly boys in order to relieve their own feelings. The whole episode cannot be better narrated than it is in the governors' order of 29 November:

> Whereas upon the 26th of this instant November some of the schollars ... being assisted by certain Townes men did presume to put in practice A violent Exclusion of theire Master to the debarring him from performeing his duty in the Schoole – And not onely so but, though they deserted the Schoole about nine of the clocke at night upon the 27th, yet about Eight of the clocke at night upon the 28th instant by the assistance of certaine (and those more) unruly persons of the Towne (in visards and with pistolls and other Armes) gathered to them and combineing with them, did make a Second assault to enter the Schoole and then and theire did not onely threaten to kill theire Master beeing gott into the Schoole but for the Space of neare two howers made such attempts by casting in Stones and bricks as well as breakeing the Wall and Wenscote of the Saide Schoole as might endanger his Life. Although for some reasons the Governors think fit their Master should pardon this present transgression in the offending schollars aforesaid, yet for those persons which from the Towne came running into such dangerous riott, tis resolved the Governours will take such course against them, as the Law provides in such Cases.

Whilst it is quite understandable that the governors should want to throw the heavy book of law at the town hooligans it is not quite as easy to see why the boys should have got off lightly – unless, of course, some of the boys were their own sons, as they are all too likely to have been. And, although these 'barrings-out' were a not uncommon feature of the vibrant life of schools at the time, a penny for Mr Brokesby's thoughts on being directed to overlook a merry frolic that might have killed him would be money well spent.

Brokesby's relations with the governors were not always easy. They had, after all, allowed him to run the school for five years (1649–54) before confirming his appointment, hardly a mark of confidence. During those years, as his letter of 19 August 1654 to the eminent Richard Baxter of Kidderminster shows, he had analysed with considerable lucidity the shortcomings in the administration of the Foundation. His analysis grew from a pet scheme to create eight scholarships, each of £10 per annum and tenable for four years, to be awarded to boys from the school who were proceeding to the university. He suggested that four should go to boys from the town, two to boys from the county of

William Wollaston taught at the school from 1683–88 and rightly identified the chicanery behind Brokesby's dismissal. In a wider sphere he was one of group of theologians propounding 'natural theology'. His main work was his *Religion of Nature Delineated.*

Warwick, one each to boys from the neighbouring counties of Worcestershire and Staffordshire. This clearly envisages using the charity for boys from outside the manor of Birmingham and this would be a radical new departure for the school, though readers will remember that the original charter was not specific as to catchment area. Brokesby's letter also reveals that he would like to see an Act of Parliament compelling funds to be provided for the regular appointment of a third schoolmaster, prohibiting governors from becoming tenants of the foundation, restricting leases to a term of twenty-one years and requiring the governors 'in setting of leases for the future to order two parts out of three of the estate ... to be reserved at an yearly rent to the school'. This, he continued, the governors 'wholly dashed out ... without any reason more than "we will get leases as we think good".' No wonder they did as he had put his finger on the ills of a hundred years. No wonder, either, that he should write that 'they must be forced or I find they will never suffer the estate to be improved'. Why, he asked, in one splendidly epigrammatic sentence, 'should ancestors' charity lie under posterity's usury?' Whether he got the moral support he was so clearly seeking from Baxter we do not know.

In 1664, ten years after Brokesby's letter to Baxter and three before the 'debarring' episode, another attack was made on what was claimed to be the inefficient and corrupt administration of the Foundation. This time, the petitioner, Mr Thomas Howard, did not suggest that foundation property and land should be handed over to the king, as Mr Nicols had done twenty-six years earlier, but that they should be handed over to him. He would guarantee £100 per annum for the affairs of the school which, he said, would be £40 per annum more than the governors allowed for that purpose. The action came before the Court of Exchequer and the Attorney-General's case was an almost point-by-point repetition of that made in 1638, with the important difference that the charge of incompetent teaching in the school was omitted. The governors' defence was detailed and thorough. They produced accounts from 1632 onwards and a transcript of their ordinances of 1596 to justify their conduct of affairs; in fact, the evidence produced in their defence has become a primary source of information about the earlier history of the Foundation. The case against them was dropped and one wonders why this cheeky take-over bid was ever made. The answer would seem to be that it was a move in a long-running war – a war which the landowning, royalist interests were prosecuting against the urban nonconformity of which the school was an expression.

Although the governors won the case it was something of a Pyrrhic victory. They could well see the way the current of national politics was running. Two expensive court actions, both probably instigated by local royalist interests, and then a destructive riot against their property by what may well have been a royalist rent-a-mob, appear to have had an intimidating effect. By the end of the 1660s the rich, influential ironmaster and governor, Humphrey Jennens, had become distinctly royalist in outlook, and several men of royalist views had been elected to the governing body. In the Orders issued on 29 November 1667, three days after the riot, was one that looks very much like being a concession to public opinion in that it prohibited anyone who had 'in present possession any lands or tenements of the said school' from being a governor. It was, of course, one of the changes that Brokesby had wished to see implemented thirteen years earlier.

In 1676 negotiations between the school and St Catherine's Hall, Cambridge, were initiated by the Bailiff, Thomas Rowney, and then conducted by Brokesby. They aimed to establish two scholarships to the college for boys from the school to be funded jointly by the college and the school. The school proposed also to found two Fellowships and the college in return to fund five other boys from Birmingham at the college. In the course of obtaining ratification of these proposals by the Court of Chancery, the governors set out the statutes and ordinances that had been agreed at a governors' meeting on 20 October 1676. Of particular importance among them are the reiterated prohibition against governors holding foundation property, the restriction of leases to twenty-one years, the establishment of the Chief Master's salary as £68.15s.0d. *per annum* and the Usher's as £34.6s.8d. per annum, the provisions for paying an assistant to the Chief Master, an assistant to the Usher and a scrivener to teach writing and 'casting accounts', the reservation of £30 per annum for maintenance of the School House and the masters' houses and the decision that surplus money should go towards scholarships to the universities. The proposals were allowed by the Chancery Court and approved by the bishop, but for various reasons the scholarship scheme was never realised and the close connection between the school and St Catherine's Hall never developed. We learn incidentally that there were at this time 'neer two hundred Schollers' in the school.

As time passed the royalist presence on the governing body increased. By 1684 when Charles required the surrender of the charter (along with many others) and promised a new one 'with such additions as might be advantageous for the promotion of learning', there were at least seven governors who were enthusiastic royalists. At a meeting on 28 June 1684, at which only eleven governors were present and which was later said to have been rigged by the royalist/Anglican group, the governors were confronted by Sir Charles Holte, Deputy Lord-Lieutenant of the County, an old boy of the school and one whose family were traditionally hostile to its governors, and on his urging they surrendered the charter. Writing of the event years later in 1709, a former Usher, William Wollaston, claimed that 'the thing was contrived by some gentlemen to bring themselves into the government of the school by turning out their old master [Brokesby] to make way for a man from Oxford who was the creature of the principal actor'. The face put upon this rebellion of the gentry, with some degree of plausibility, was that the governing body was corrupt and inefficient. They were to claim later that the old governors being 'of mean degree and estate made leases to one another of the school lands much under value'. In a later lawsuit they were to assert that Charles II 'resolved to take the management out of the hands of such mean, necessitous persons and vest it in others whose quality and fortunes placed them above the temptation of misemploying the charity'. The assumption in the last sentence would seem to be hasty and optimistic to say the least of it and reveals very clearly the class basis of the changes that were taking place on the governing body.

Although Charles II died on 6 February 1685 before the new charter was issued, it was granted by his brother, James, about a fortnight later on 22 February. The new charter named a new group of governors, thirteen in number, of whom six were from the old governing body (needless to say the royalist group), five were local gentry and two were neighbouring clerics, the incumbents at Northfield and Yardley. It was a good balance between town and gentry and it broke, as it was meant to, the overall control of school affairs by the town oligarchy. The new charter was in many respects a repetition of the old but there were significant changes, several – but not all – for the better.

Seal used by the 'New Governors'.

Governors would not be allowed to own or lease foundation property; free places were to be limited to boys from the town and manor of Birmingham; the endowment could be used for the upkeep of buildings as well as teacher's salaries; there should be three masters; the Chief Master and the Usher must be in Holy Orders; the Chief Master must be at least an MA and the Usher at least a BA. These last two requirements look as if they were specially designed to get rid of Brokesby and they support the charge later made by Woolaston and quoted above. They were certainly used successfully for that purpose. In future the Bailiff was to be called President, thereby removing from his office the appearance of being principally a rent-collector and property manager; one cannot help thinking that that was how many previous bailiffs had seen their office. There was, finally, one alarming provision in the new charter – that the king constituted himself Visitor of the school with power to dismiss the President or any governor or master as he pleased. The Crown was going to make sure that the link between the school and Birmingham's stroppy nonconformity was broken.

Brokesby was an immediate casualty of the new charter. It was said that in his later years as Chief Master his effectiveness had declined. It was, nevertheless, hard that after thirty-six years of efficient and creative leadership – about fifty boys sent to the universities, a vigilant watch kept on the repair of the buildings, a library built to house the collection of books begun in Barton's time, imaginative schemes for scholarships to the universities and for boys in the school – it was hard to be turned off for no very sufficient reason. His independence of mind and the fact that he nagged the governors to keep the foundation buildings in proper repair probably did not endear him to them, and as they became increasingly royalist in sympathy his links with nonconformity probably did him no good either. So with the choice between a lump sum of £40 or a pension of £20 for the first year and £10 for each subsequent year they sent him back home to Leicestershire, where he took care to die within two years and was the winner by securing £40 for two years and not £30 as he would have done had he made the alternative choice. He also omitted to leave a large sum of money (£400–£700) to the Foundation as he had intended. Perhaps at sixty-five Brokesby should have been thinking that enough was enough but the manner of his going leaves a nasty taste.

It is clear that by this time the existence of a Petty School (or English School) was an established fact. Its function was as a preparatory school to the grammar school. In it boys were taught to read and write, and orders passed by the new governors on 28 January 1686 are concerned with its organisation. Each year boys shall move up from the Petty School to the Grammar School. The Petty School should never exceed forty boys and never more than twenty 'upon the Founder's Charity'. Certificates of parental poverty under the hands of at least two governors were required before a boy could be admitted.

The new Chief Master, John Hickes, whom the new governors installed was a Fellow of Magdalen College, Oxford. 'Creature' or not, he was not a bad Chief Master though his period of office was short. It was short because the regime of the new governors was short, and that was short for the most bizarre of reasons. Their installation had never been accepted by those of the old governors who had not been appointed to the new governing body and who continued to meet and to consider themselves as governors. After the departure of James II they began to think of counter-attack and found, no doubt to their delight, that the surrender of the old charter had never been properly enrolled and consequently the new charter was invalid and the governors whom it appointed were illegitimate. To cut not only a long story but a deal of tedious litigation short the old governors were, by 1692, finally reinstated. Their Whiggish nonconformity was more grateful to William's government than the Jacobite proclivities of their erstwhile supplanters. The new charter was abrogated and another Chief Master appointed but it took a further two years to force Hickes to vacate the school building and his own house. This was finally achieved in 1694.

Two years after Hickes had come to Birmingham the Fellows of Magdalen College, Oxford elected an Old Edwardian, John Hough, as their President, against the wishes of James II. The Fellows refused to elect the king's nominee and Hough refused to go. He survived after the king's flight to remain President until 1699, in the meantime becoming Bishop of Oxford, later translated to Lichfield and then to Worcester. He declined the Primacy that he was offered on the death of Archbishop Tenison in 1715. He is undoubtedly one of the most

John Hough (1651–1743).

27

admirable of the school's alumni and he readily acknowledged his debt to Brokesby. His integrity was celebrated later, in 1738, when Pope made him an exemplar of that staunch quality in the *Epilogue to the Satires, Dialogue II*.

> There other Trophies deck the truly Brave
> . . . .
> Such as on HOUGH'S unsully'd Mitre shine
> Or beam, good DIGBY! from a Heart like thine.

It is interesting that the Digby whom Pope brackets with Hough was also connected with King Edward's School. He was the fourth Baron Digby and was made a governor of the school in 1687 at the age of twenty-five and his elder brother, Simon, the third baron, had actually been a boy at the school. Pope's own note on Hough and Digby reads 'the one an assertor of the Church of England in opposition to the false measures of King James II. The other as firmly attached to the cause of that king. Both acting out of principle, and equally men of honour and virtue.'

One feels that those at the Birmingham School who wanted to get on with education would have sighed in sympathy with the lines that Dryden was to write in the spring of 1700, in the last weeks of his life as he looked back over the century that was coming to a close:

> 'Tis well an old age is out,
> And time to begin a new.

But the old wrangles were not over and were to disturb the first quarter of the new century.

28

3

Greek Meets Greek

When GEORGE in pudding-time came o'er
And moderate men looked big, sir,
I turned a cat-in-pan once more
And so became a Whig, sir.

The Vicar of Bray

THE EVENTS RELATING to the abrogation and subsequent reinstatement of the old Charter demonstrate that schools are no more cocooned from the prevailing currents of opinion than any other institution. The Whig tide that in 1715 brought George over 'in pudding-time' had set in 'when William was our king declared' in 1688, the Toryism of Anne's reign notwithstanding. In 1692, with the appointment of James Parkinson as master of the Free Grammar School of Birmingham the governors anticipated the *Vicar of Bray* by upwards of twenty years. This appointment was strongly supported by Archbishop Tillotson, deistically inclined and so likely to be Whig in sympathy, and by John Somers, a brilliant Whig lawyer who was later to become William III's Lord Chancellor and the most able and influential of Whig spokesmen. It may be worth noting that in the legal manoeuvring to invalidate the new charter and to reinstate the old governors the latter had employed Somers. In 1694 Hickes was finally ejected and a new order, which was really the old order, began.

James Parkinson is the first Chief Master whose character comes down to us in three-dimensional technicolour. He was described as 'a little man, very furious and fiery' and before arriving in Birmingham his career had certainly not lacked colour. He had graced with his somewhat fleeting presence four Oxford colleges – Brasenose, Corpus Christi, Gloucester Hall and Hart Hall – before being elected a Fellow of Lincoln College in 1674. By all accounts he was an excellent college tutor, a good scholar and a stimulating and conscientious teacher. He was at the same time, however, one 'of whom divers men had different apprehensions'. He was irrepressibly vocal on political topics, always 'discoursing of state affairs', an extreme exclusionist, one who always took the opposite view,

29

just the type to be the delight of his students and the *bête noire* of most of his colleagues. Seen through the Tory eyes of the eighteenth-century antiquary, Thomas Hearne, he was:

> a rank, stinking Whig, who used to defend the murder of King Charles I and recommend Milton and other Republican rascals to his pupils ... This Parkinson, when the factious townsmen of Birmingham had got their honest School Master Mr Hickes unjustly turned out ... was the man that ... Tillotson treacherously imposed upon them. In King William's reign (when the sneaking villains, like worms upon a rain, crawled out of their lurking holes) he appeared in print in a small Pamphlet against Dr Tim. Halton, the Vice Chancellor.

He was accused of claiming that 'the King might be for ever laid aside so there should never be King in England for the future'. As a result he had been deprived of his Fellowship and expelled, in a not entirely straightforward way, from his college and from Oxford. But it is not surprising that he should have been seen as acceptable to Archbishop Tillotson and to the independently-minded, reinstated old governors of King Edward's School, though it is unlikely that the latter could have imagined quite what was coming to them.

Parkinson's Chief Mastership ran fairly quietly for a few years. From the start, though, he seems to have viewed expenditure on such matters as repairs and building as an extravagant, not to say illegal, diversion of Foundation income from its proper purpose, to wit the salaries of himself and his Usher, Josiah Foster. Yet it was not until Mr Samuel Eden, a Birmingham lawyer who had handled with some efficiency the case for the old governors during the protracted reinstatement litigation, was elected as a governor that open warfare began. If the events of the Smalbroke – Colmore feud of a hundred years earlier occasionally remind one of a Hollywood western, those in the first two decades of the eighteenth century resemble nothing so much as one of those long-running soap operas in which the characters unfailingly act like quarrelsome babies.

Eden resembled Richard Smalbroke in being a tough, domineering personality of considerable ability and he quickly established his control over the other governors. In the course of the case that Parkinson was to bring against the governors in 1710 his mother-in-law, Sarah Freher, deposed that once, when Parkinson had asked one of the governors, Mr Careless, 'why it was that the governors allowed themselves to be ruled by Mr. Sam. Eden' Careless had answered, 'Lord, Sir, what would you have me do, when we are in the hands of the cut-throat we must humour him till we get out of his clutches.' At the same hearing, Josiah Foster deposed that when he had once asked Mr Eden if he had threatened Mr Parkinson that he would break down the school door if Mr Parkinson locked it against him, Eden had said, 'Do you side with Parkinson? I will not only break open the school but the houses too and set fire to them, by God.' When Foster reproved him for swearing Eden said, 'Shall I be talked to by such a pusillanimous and pitiful fellow as you are?' and then used 'a great deal of scurrilous and abusive language'. Parkinson was equally choleric. We learn from the deposition of Humfrey Cookes, the master of the English School, that one day 'Mr. Parkinson came into the English School in a hasty and violent manner and drove out the scholars' and also that Mr Cookes 'had heard

Mr. Parkinson hint or express himself in a "big manner" as if the whole of the revenue of the School belonged to him and the Usher'.

The governors' orders for 28 August 1702 are evidence of their determination to control Parkinson. They record that an increase in salary for both Parkinson and Foster was to be continued 'during our pleasure' (an ominous qualification) and that every two months the Bailiff and governors should visit the school 'to rectify what they shall find amiss therein'. They had Parkinson in their sights, and the related issues of the disposal of foundation revenue, masters' salaries and building plans were the focal points of what was obviously a power struggle between Parkinson and Eden. In 1705 when Parkinson's observations became too splenetic to be borne the governors ordered 'that the additional salaries viz. £20 p. ann. to Mr Parkinson and £10 p. ann. to Mr. Foster shall be taken away and held at Mich. next and so for the future'. They also appointed a new assistant in the grammar school at £20 per annum, a Mr John Bridgeman, a decision that Parkinson may well have seen as being aimed at him. The governors were anxious to proceed with repair and building work and this involved the Chief Master's house as well as the school buildings, but, whether by oversight or design, they omitted to let Parkinson know of this. Consequently, when in 1707 he returned from a visit to London, he found half his house pulled down. In 1708 the governors decided to stop paying the window tax on the masters' houses and this, for Parkinson, was the last straw. He presented a Bill of Complaint to the Lord Chancellor which, in its turn, provoked the governors to decide to sack him. As might be expected, they alleged his 'mismanagement, unquietness and unfitness to be Chief Master' and ordered 'an ejectment to be prosecuted against him'. Yet Parkinson remained in office for a further fourteen years because the old charter, so lovingly restored, gave no power to the governors to get rid of obstreperous Chief Masters. What the governors had joined no man could put asunder.

Between 1710 and 1726 a great deal of the Foundation's dirty linen was washed in public. The intricate tangle of issues and personalities exhibited during this process achieves the impenetrable density of which only the legal affairs of King Edward's School in its first 170 years were capable. Two main strands emerge, however; the first is the ramification of Parkinson's personal quarrel with the governors, and the second is the can of worms opened by the Royal Commission that was constituted in 1722 following a petition by sixteen inhabitants of Birmingham, citizens who were suspiciously closely linked with Eden's enemies on the governing body.

To simplify the mass of detailed points that surfaced as a consequence of Parkinson's suit against the governors his case rested upon his claim that the governors had failed to implement some of the prescriptions of their own ordinance of 1676. They had not funded exhibitions to the universities or the scheme to finance poor apprentices and they had not, prior to their demolition programme in the first decade of the eighteenth century, seen to repairs to the masters' houses, even though the Statutes of 1676 had stipulated that £30 a year should be reserved for maintenance work on existing buildings. But, claimed Parkinson, the Statutes had said nothing about expenditure on new buildings.

John Somers, a leading whig lawyer and later Lord Chancellor to William III, a supporter of Parkinson.

His case was that these purposes had a prior claim on the Foundation income to that of new building. The governors' defence was based on the assertions that their rebuilding plans had the approval of many of the town's inhabitants, that Parkinson was as well paid as any schoolmaster and that he was not really justifying his large salary as the school under his control was going downhill. This latter point had largely to do with numbers. They certainly seem to have been dropping, and this can be attributed partly to Parkinson's noted severity with his pupils and partly to the fact that his notorious Whiggery predisposed local gentlemen to send their sons to other nearby schools – Rugby, Stratford, Alcester and the new school at Solihull. As for his severity, his methods may have suited some boys, the minority who managed to be both able and tough, but it was not unknown for boys who had settled quite happily in the lower forms in the school simply to refuse to continue to attend when they became the Chief Master's pupils.

The fact that many fewer boys went on to the universities during Parkinson's reign was not, however, entirely his fault. The governors were also to blame because after Brokesby's departure they had shown no interest in his scheme for school exhibitions to Cambridge and Oxford and had thus effectively closed the universities to poor boys. This situation, combined with the fact that Parkinson's politics induced the gentry to send their sons elsewhere, reduced to a minimum the number of Edwardians going on to the universities. Whatever the rights and wrongs of this particular issue litigation ground on for several years to a stalemate, in spite of the intervention of Lord Somers on Parkinson's behalf. The outcome was that the latter regained his increase of salary and received some reimbursement of his legal costs but had to continue paying his window tax and his own house repairs. The governors continued to ignore the funding of exhibitions and of poor apprentices but seem to have halted building work. But most important Parkinson remained Chief Master for several years until his death in 1722.

During this period Parkinson figured in an episode which exemplifies the close involvement of the school in the life of the town, this time its religious life. In the first decade of the eighteenth century it was proposed to build a large new church in Birmingham. The bishop of the diocese was the distinguished Old Edwardian, John Hough, mentioned in the previous chapter. His devotion to the interests of the Church of England and his consequent suspicion of the Dissenting tradition of Birmingham led him to write to Lord Somers that 'if it be left to me ... there shall not be one Townsman' among those commissioned to supervise the building of the new church. He would have only 'persons of the best Quality and best Character', in other words the local gentry whose Church of England loyalties could be relied on. Hough's correspondence shows, too, that he had tried and failed to induce the school governors to settle a pension 'out of school rents' upon the incumbent of the new church 'for his better maintenance'. This, of course, would have been outside the terms of the school's charter. It takes little imagination to envisage the volcanic scale of Parkinson's explosion had the proposal been implemented, particularly as the first incumbent, the Revd William Higgs, turned out, not unexpectedly, to be a combative Tory

PLATE 3 The Upper Corridor of Barry's Building, painted by Mrs Ravenhill. It was moved stone-by-stone to the new school site at Edgbaston and modified to become the Memorial Chapel (*inset*).

PLATE 4 'Sun, Wind & Rain', by David Cox (1783 – 1859). David Cox is known to have been a pupil of Joseph Barber, for some time drawing master of King Edward's School, and to have attended the school himself for a short time.

High Churchman. In 1715 the new Church of St Philip was consecrated and in the same year religious riots broke out in Birmingham, sparked by the preaching of Dr Sacheverel, a rabble-rousing High Church divine. The situation is marvellously described in William Hutton's *An History of Birmingham* (1781):

> In 1688, when the nation chose to expel a race of kings ... our peaceable sons of art ... smiled with the rest of the nation at the landing of the Prince of Orange, and exerted their little assistance towards effecting the Revolution ... In the reign of Queen Anne, when that flaming luminary, Dr. Sacheverel, set half the kingdom in blaze, the inhabitants of this region of industry caught the spark of the day, and grew warm for the church ... As the doctor rode in triumph through the streets of Birmingham, this flimsy idol of party snuffed up the incense of the populace, but the more sensible withheld their homage; and when he preached at Sutton Coldfield ... the people of Birmingham crowded in multitudes round his pulpit. But it does not appear that he taught his hearers to build up Zion, but perhaps to pull her down; for they immediately went and gutted a meeting-house.

They seem to have had the tacit approval of the Rector of St Philip's. In the following year, December 1716, Parkinson's son delivered, in the school, an oration written by his father and called *A Loyal Oration*. It was a Whiggish call-to-arms, a tissue of lurid, anti-Catholic rhetoric, forcefully written and empty of thought. It offended Mr Higgs, who attacked it in a sermon from his own pulpit, and it called from John Bridgeman, formerly assistant master at the school and now Vicar of Aston, an equally polemical reply. Preached on 30 January 1717, the anniversary day of the execution of Charles I and published later in the year, his discourse was predictably entitled *The Martyrdom of King Charles the First*. Parkinson riposted with a pamphlet, *A Letter to the Reverend Mr. Higgs, Rector of St. Philip's Church in Birmingham*. The title is hardly fiery but in the eighteenth century you never knew what lurked behind a harmless title. In this case it was a dozen pages of relentlessly repetitive polemic that proved and reproved and proved again that Mr Higgs seditiously avoided, by various despicable Jacobite subterfuges, actually praying for our gracious Hanoverian

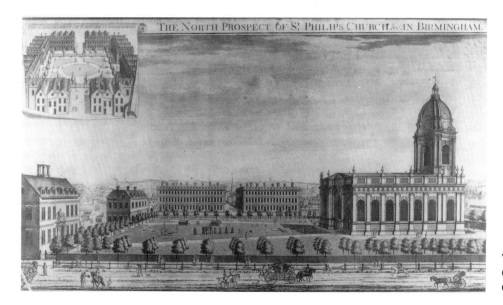

The north prospect of St Philip's Church, now Birmingham Cathedral.

king. The spectacle of the Chief Master of the school locked in polemical combat with his former assistant and a brother Anglican clergyman may well have afforded amusement to the more irreverent spirits in the town. In this incident, the school can be seen as a microcosm of the religious passions of the time, a time when, as Joseph Hill put it 'the firebrand followers of Sacheverel ... had burnt nonconformist chapels in and around Birmingham and were covertly encouraged and condoned by clergymen holding pulpits in the leading churches; and ... the nonconformists, whose existence was tolerated on sufferance, could produce champions as choleric and almost as intolerant as Sacheverel himself.'

The troubles of the school did not cease with Parkinson's death in March 1722. As his successor the governors appointed John Hausted who had applied unsuccessfully for the post of Usher when it had fallen vacant two years previously. He had been the candidate of Samuel Eden but on that occasion Eden had been outwitted or, as he saw it, betrayed. A fellow governor, John Greene, on whose support Eden thought that he could rely, at the crucial meeting not only proposed and voted for an alternative candidate but lobbied several other governors to do the same. The alternative candidate was Greene's grandson, Thomas, and he was duly appointed as Usher. This led to a bitter internal battle between the Eden and Greene factions on the governing body and to Eden making life hell for Thomas Greene, not least by refusing to pay his salary. Each party to the dispute took the other to court and finally the Greene faction secured the appointment of a Royal Commission which began work in November 1722, eight months after Parkinson's death, and reported in May 1723.

Its conclusions were far from flattering to the management of the Foundation. It found that several governors, including Eden, had not been properly eligible for election and consequently Hausted's appointment, along with many other decisions, was invalid; that three successive Ushers, Foster, Pipe and Greene, had been persecuted and driven to law by Eden; that a deal of financial sharp-practice had taken place; that Eden had illegally retained the governors' seal for fifteen years and that for twenty years no exhibitions to the universities had been provided by the governors for boys from the school. As far as Eden was concerned the writing on the wall was plain to see, but he did not immediately surrender; he claimed that for technical legal reasons (he was, after all, a smart lawyer himself) the commission was illegal. But his arguments cut no ice with the Lord Chancellor and 1726 saw the end of Eden as a power in the affairs of the school. Hausted, who appears to have been a decent man caught up in an intricate and vicious wrangle that was not of his making, resigned and retired to open a private grammar school at Deritend where he was Vicar of St John's.

With the passing of Parkinson and Eden, and the management of school affairs fumigated by the Royal Commission, we come to the end of what might be called the heroic age of the Foundation, heroic because most of the personalities involved behaved with the aggressive and uncomplicated egotism of epic characters. No small task faced Hausted's successor, the task of restoring to the school something of the excellence that it had known under Brokesby and Hickes.

4

The Big Sleep?

Sleep after toyle, port after stormie seas,
Ease after war, death after life, does greatly please.

Edmund Spenser: *The Faerie Queene*

'Sir, (said Johnson) in Lichfield we are a city of philosophers, we work with our heads, and make the boobies of Birmingham work for us with their hands.'

James Boswell: *Life of Johnson*

CONVENTIONAL WISDOM often presents the eighteenth century as time of slumbrous educational inertia. So general a notion, however, does not bear close examination and as the century developed the 'boobies of Birmingham' (in Johnson's combative yet jocular phrase) showed a capacity to use their heads to some purpose. This was so even in the case of the Free Grammar School and though, as we shall see, the dichotomy between heads and hands became more pronounced as the century drew to its close, the Foundation tried to do its duty by both.

In the years following Parkinson's death and Eden's overdue disappearance into well-merited obscurity the governors grappled with problems which had bedevilled them for a long time, problems that had been created by the original Charter. The formulation of the Charter's provisions was precise in a way that made it unintentionally restrictive. It specified a single school, staffed by one master and one usher but made no provision for development. This meant that if the governors wished to enlarge the teaching body or repair or replace buildings they laid themselves open to the charge of misusing Foundation income. We have seen that, on the one hand, Brokesby had to nag consistently for money to be spent on repairs and, on the other, Parkinson was able to argue from the terms of the Charter that surplus income, derived from the rise in land and property values resulting from the town's growth, should properly be used to increase masters' salaries. But it was common sense that a larger town meant more boys and more boys meant more teachers and larger buildings and that building extensions need money. Common sense, however, is not a legal

'The Free School', in the early eighteenth century. An engraving from *A History of Birmingham* by William Hutton, 1781.

35

argument and so it is not difficult to see that the letter of the Charter could be used by anyone who, for one reason or another, wanted to impede the expansion of the school. It had been clear in Brokesby's time that the needs of the town were not fully met by the educational programme of the traditional grammar school, and that this situation had been at least partly remedied by setting up the English School and by the appointment of a writing-master. No serious objections had been made to these developments but the governors ran into trouble when they tried seriously to tackle the problem of buildings.

It was the erection, in 1702–4, of a new building for the English School that brought violent opposition from the Chief Master and was the seed from which his prolonged quarrels with the governors grew. In 1707 these burst into luxuriant flower when the governors ordered that 'the other part of the school shall be built this year according to the form of the English School'. Some unsatisfactory new building took place but the legal wrangles between Chief Master and governors, precipitated by this rebuilding, delayed a full-scale rebuilding plan for twenty years. Once Parkinson was dead, however, and his successor, the unhappy Hausted, had been moved along to labour in a neighbouring corner of the Lord's educational vineyard at Deritend, the governors could once again turn their thoughts to buildings. At a governors' meeting on 4 May 1731 it was ordered that 'the present Bailiff do cause the said school to be pulled down and rebuilt and also the Usher's house'. The wording is terse and the instruction comprehensive – a complete rebuilding to be undertaken. A little less than three years later the orders and resolutions following the governors' meeting on 18 January 1734 record that 'the rebuilding of the said school and the houses of the Chief Master and Usher are almost completed'. While the building work was in progress the work of the school went on in a hired room until enough of the new building had been erected to make its use possible. The acounts for 1731 record that 10s. 6d. was paid 'for a room to teach in'. It was not the last time in the history of the school that temporary accommodation had to be found so that lessons could continue while a new school was being built.

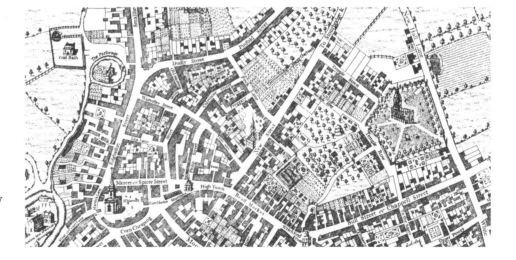

Birmingham in 1731. The map records that in the first thirty years of the eighteenth century the number of streets almost doubled from 30 to 55, 1215 new houses were built and the town's population rose from 15,032 to over 23,000.

The Georgian school, the New Street front. From a print in the possession of the Governors.

The new building was to be erected on the site of the old. It is unfortunate that no representation of the mediaeval Guild Hall exists but T. W. Hutton suggests that the Guild Hall still standing today at nearby Henley-in-Arden gives us a good idea of what it may have looked like – a simple, timber-framed, wattle-and-daub structure. If surviving drawings are anything to go by its successor was an attractive, two-storey building, the overall elegance of which was only slightly spoiled by a rather comic little clock-tower which was perched on top of a small, lower tower above the main entrance. In a niche on the front wall of this lower tower was a statue (for which the governors paid £25) of King Edward VI holding ball and sceptre. But if the presence of the clock-tower disturbed the harmony of the total design it also gave a distinctive look to the building's front elevation. The ground plan was the familiar post-Renaissance one where two wings, projecting from a central block, enclose a courtyard which is open on the fourth side, in this case fronting New Street. Some years after the completion of this building a library was added at the back of the structure. All that survives from this Georgian building is an imposing marble fireplace (now in the present Governors' Room) for which the governors paid E. Scheemakers of Vine Street, Piccadilly, the sum of £87.1s.0d. Of the alternative designs that Mr Scheemakers submitted the governors prudently chose the cheaper. A watercolour of the 'Great School' of this Georgian building breathes a relaxed atmosphere that has the appearance of a private study period in any school at any time. One is not immediately struck by an impression of energetic, purposeful study. One boy is sitting casually on the step of a large desk, 'minding his book' as his master would have put it; another is whipping a top; a third, occupying the foreground and looking rather more senior than the others, leans listlessly against a desk, his book depending from a languid hand as he idly watches his eyelashes grow. It is a picture with much to attract those of us who live in a more vibrant educational climate.

The rebuilding of the main school buildings took place during the Chief Mastership of Edward Mainwaring who had succeeded Hausted in 1726. Like all previous holders of his position except Brokesby he was in holy orders, and his conception of his Chief Masterly function focuses an important question – that of Chief Masterly absence. The governors who had introduced the short-lived new charter in 1685 had ruled that no Chief Master should at the same time hold any clerical appointment, a requirement that was complementary to their insistence that the Chief Master should be a cleric, and a safeguard against the

'Great School' in Georgian times, from a watercolour by Samuel Lines.

pluralist habit that was deeply rooted in ecclesiastical tradition. This wise precaution, however, had not been retained when the old charter had been restored. No problems had arisen with either Hickes or Parkinson, both of whom apparently saw themselves as schoolmasters *et praeterea nihil*, but Mainwaring evidently felt that it was possible to combine a cure of souls with a cure of youthful minds, especially as he had a very competent and willing second-in-command in Thomas Greene. So we find in the governors' orders for 7 December 1737 the carefully unspecific but revealing entry: 'It is ordered that the present Bailiff do pay unto Mr. Thomas Greene ten pounds as a gratuity to him for his extraordinary attendance upon the service of the said school in the absence of the Chief Master.' Almost identical entries appear in the orders for 3 May 1738, 4 April 1739 and 3 October 1739 after which Greene's salary appears to have been formally increased by £20 per annum, thereby rendering further *ad hoc* supplements unnecessary. It would, perhaps, be unjust to suppose that

Mainwaring gave all his time to his alternative responsibilities; he probably looked in on King Edward's School from time to time to make sure that Greene was doing his job.

The governors were clearly unhappy about the situation and so, one imagines, were Greene and Mainwaring's assistant, Perks. One may wonder why Mainwaring was not simply dismissed. However, the governors' record in this delicate area was not impressive. Admittedly they had succeeded in demoting (but not dismissing) the aged Billingsley nearly a century before, but it had taken them two years to get rid of Hickes, an achievement they were unable to repeat in Parkinson's case after fourteen years of trying. There is a wry irony in the fact that their only completely successful dismissal had been that of the best Chief Master they had ever had – Brokesby. So they tried to redeploy the teaching power of the school and apparently sought confirmation of their proposals, as it was proper for them to do, from the bishop. A letter from him to one of the governors suggests, in the unintentionally expressive felicity of one muddling and labyrinthine sentence, the absurdity of the case upon which he was asked to adjudicate. So confused was his lordship by the situation that he consistently referred to Mr Perks as Mr Parker.

Oct. 13th 1733

Sir,
Not doubting but that Mr. Parker in consequence of his visit to me here, intimated to you and your brethren my disposition to concur with you in your scheme for restoring the credit and prosperity of Birmingham School, I shall now only add that though, by way of trial of the projected temporal provision for so doing, Mr. Greene and Mr. Parker may be employed as you have proposed; yet a just precaution ought to be used on this occasion: namely, that as Mr. Greene is not to be really invested with the post of Head-Schoolmaster, to the prejudice, and indeed the exclusion, of Mr. Mainwaring who is so; so likewise Mr. Parker is not to be chose usher at present, since Mr. Greene is really so, and continues to be so, notwithstanding he is allowed to be a temporary substitute to Mr. Mainwaring.

One must admire the cautiously diplomatic way in which the bishop keeps his escape routes open yet at the same time conceals the fact in the convolutions of his sentence structure. As a result Mainwaring continued to draw his salary for another thirteen years until he died in 1746 while Greene and Perks soldiered on, for most of the time doing a job one level above that for which they were being paid. When teaching was the Chief Master's primary function and he contributed a fifth to a quarter of the total teaching power of the school his absence would have been more noticeable than in times when his talents are expected to be exercised on administration and public relations. Yet the work of the school went on with no evident diminution of efficiency, largely, one supposes, as a result of the energy and ability of Thomas Greene. In fact, this is nearly always so in cases of headmasterly absence. Certainly, today, with vastly larger common-rooms and headmasters often required to appear on television or give their advice at innumerable meetings of national importance, their absence does not in any way affect the daily running of the school. It is the Second Master or Deputy Head (the Usher in days gone by) who, like the First Lieutenant in HM ships, oversees the smooth running of daily routine, and it is the assistant masters who actually have daily contact with the boys and whose ideas and example most influence them.*

On Mainwaring's death in 1746 the governors passed over Thomas Greene's claims to succeed him, based as they were merely on twenty-six years' devoted and reliable service to the Foundation. The governors seem, however, to have been under some pressure. By this time they were inclining to establishment, High Church interests, a development to be discussed later. John Wilkinson's credentials were impeccable – Eton, Senior Fellow of Emmanuel College, Cambridge, Rector of Wallington, Herts. It is fairly clear that his stipend at Wallington was inadequate to his requirements. In his letter of application he explains that 'having unluckily trusted my whole fortune in a relation's hands, and being further bound to him for several sums, I was (through his failure) plunged into unforeseen difficulties, which I happily got over in a little time, and have been ever since in Sir Robert Lawley's family, private tutor to his son.' His employment in Sir Robert's household was, in its nature, temporary and it was time to look for something permanent. Sir Robert seconded his application with a letter of recommendation to the governors in which he wrote: 'I have great hopes of Mr. Wilkinson's success, especially as his character and capacity are already known to both Mr. Vyse and Mr. Dovey, whose opinions will probably have great weight with the other governors.' (Mr Vyse and Mr Dovey were both clerical governors, the first such for many a year.) To make sure that the governors were in no doubt that Wilkinson was the man to choose Sir Robert added: 'I have taken the freedom to trouble you with a letter, and am persuaded you will at my request use your best endeavours to serve him.' The phrase 'at my request' carries uncomfortable overtones of Goneril's threat to her father:

> Be then desired
> By her, who else will take the thing she begs

During Wilkinson's thirteen years at the school he and Greene between them sent fourteen scholars to Oxford or Cambridge on school exhibitions, nine being Wilkinson's pupils and five Greene's. Like most of the other Chief Masters Wilkinson was a thoroughly competent classics teacher but apparently he never learned to manage money. Even with two incomes, one from the school and one from his parish, it was necessary that after his death the governors should order, at a meeting of 2 May 1759, that the Bailiff 'do pay into the hands of the trustees of the late Mr. John Wilkinson to whom he made over his estate and effects for the benefit of his creditors the sum of thirty-six pounds, nineteen shillings and seven pence for so much of his salary as was owing to him at the time of his death as Chief Master of the said school.'

The governors had never been ungenerous to the teaching body though on one or two occasions early in the life of the school they had needed reminding of the facts of life, and it is good to see them on this occasion so quick to accept their responsibilities to one who had died in their service. Wilkinson appears to have been a well-liked man and, eleven years after his death, was the subject of a splendid example of eighteenth-century occasional verse which T. W. Hutton has rescued for us from Aris's *Birmingham Magazine*:

* See Appendix 2.

40

Oh Wilkinson how fresh they memory flows
Through fading time, and like a lily grows,
Still ripening more as rolling years run on
While Merit owns thee for her darling son.
Arise, Great Shade, and view the annual Feast
Where bumpers rouse thee from thy peaceful rest.

The 'annual Feast' seems to have been a kind of Old Boys' Dinner which
Wilkinson's former pupils had inaugurated in the year of his death, a fact which
suggests that he had been a popular and successful schoolmaster, though it must
be admitted that the eighteenth-century 'man of sense' needed little excuse for
a bumper or two.

On Wilkinson's death Thomas Greene at last came into what he doubtless felt
was his inheritance. After thirty-nine years as Usher he was finally appointed
Chief Master at the age of sixty-two. To appoint a man of his age was quite an
unusual decision, as until the twentieth century such appointments went more
often to younger rather than older men, quite often to very young men indeed.
Greene's appointment furnishes us with a nice example of the caution, already
alluded to, which the restrictive nature of the Charter induced in those
responsible for the administration of the Foundation. Three months after
Greene's appointment the governors resolved, in a particularly enlightened
moment, to 'pay unto the said Chief Master one hundred and ten pounds for
some books bought of him for the use of the library belonging to the same
school'. They then quite properly sought ratification of their decision from the
bishop. The caution of his reply exemplifies for us the way in which the Charter
constricted decision-making, even in so obviously an internal matter as this:

Edgbaston Hall and Pool in the
eighteenth century.

> Sir,
> Please give my compliments to the governors of the school, acquainting them that I
> have perused the catalogue of the books you sent me, and approve very much of their
> design to purchase them. But as I have neither the Statutes nor the Decretal Orders by
> me, I am not prepared to give my consent to it, not knowing how far our united power
> will extend in this respect. I suppose it can be no prejudice, either to the buyer or the
> seller of the books, if this business should be postponed till I return into the country.
> I will then peruse the Statutes &c., and shall very readily give my consent to the
> purchase if I find myself at liberty to do so; and if not, it will be easy for me then to
> propose a question for the opinion of some able counsellor which may soon be
> obtained. Uninformed as I am at present it would be in vain to attempt any such thing.
> > I am, Sir
> > Yours Ac.,
> > Fred: Lich: & Cov:

Greene's reign as Chief Master lasted until his death in 1766 after forty-six years
in harness at the school. He is not a figure who occupies the foreground very
much after the initial squabbles concerning his appointment as Usher and his
subsequent persecution by Samuel Eden. But one may conjecture that his overall
contribution to the life of the school was certainly no less than that of some of
the more charismatic personalities who were to follow him in the next century.
Readiness to get on with the job without making a song and dance about it may
not be a fashionable trait of character but it is none the less admirable for that.

As the eighteenth century proceeded the nature of the education that the school offered was a matter of increasing concern. There had been the hint as far back as 1638, at the hearing before the Court of Exchequer, that many of the honest citizenry of Birmingham might wish their children to be brought up for trade rather than to aim at a university. The establishment of the Petty School, where the English master taught reading and the Scrivener taught writing and 'the casting of accounts', had been the governors' response to the situation in the seventeenth century. But their concern reappeared in the eighteenth century and we find that at their meeting on 7 September 1743 they decided to appoint a mathematics teacher as an assistant to the Scrivener. They recognised that a 'skilful and industrious ... writing master is a great benefit and advantage to the inhabitants of the ... town' and by increasing the Scrivener's salary they enabled him to pay 'an assistant for teaching mathematics'. There is little doubt that the principal function of the mathematics master was to teach 'the casting of accounts', an activity close to the town's increasingly commercial and manufacturing heart.

The men who were making the wheels of Birmingham go round increasingly saw a classical education as irrelevant to the future that they proposed for their sons. And of those sons who did, in fact, pass through the Grammar School and follow its classical curriculum, to which by its Charter it was bound, not all that many were prepared to continue such a course at the university which, in its turn, offered nothing else. Revealingly enough, after about 1760 the governors themselves, though continuing to educate their sons at the school, did not seem interested in sending them to the universities. After 1759, no exhibition went to a governor's son for the rest of the century and few of them went to the university without an exhibition. The universities had small attraction for many Birmingham parents and were becoming, more and more, places for the sons of gentry and those of the middle classes who saw the mark of a gentleman in the time-honoured way as one who eschewed trade and manual activity. But the number of sons of gentry coming to the school had declined. Since the ejection of the gentry-dominated New Charter governors in the early 1690s, followed by the reign of a 'rank, stinking Whig', followed by a period presided over by a largely absentee Chief Master, local gentlemen had found it hard to view the school with enthusiasm. So by the second half of the eighteenth century those boys who did proceed to the universities were likely to be the sons of clergy or professional men, and the governors were becoming aware that the income from their endowments was gradually ceasing to cater for the educational needs of Birmingham.

At their meeting of 6 March 1751 the governors took a bold and public-spirited decision.* It was to open four elementary schools in several parts of the town where boys and girls would be taught to read and write by teachers of both sexes. Classes were not to exceed forty and the teachers were to be paid £15 a year; this amount was to be reduced when the classes were not up to strength, a system of payment by numbers rather than that of payment by results, so beloved of liberal economists a hundred years later. The governors were anxious 'to extend the said charity as far as in us lies', a refreshing thought. It appears

John Brailsford, Chief Master (1766–75).

* See Appendix 3.

to have been the governors' intention that these classes should take place in the houses of the teachers because in that way they would circumvent the Charter's prescription that there should be one school. Moreover, they could then locate the schools where they felt the need to be greatest simply by appointing as teachers people who lived in that particular area.

Strictly speaking the elementary schools are not part of the history of the Free Grammar School. But they indicate clearly – as do the additional grammar schools that the Foundation was to establish towards the end of the nineteenth century – a consistent factor in the governors' understanding of the Foundation's purpose. They saw, rightly, that it existed for Birmingham and its priority must always be the educational interests of the town and its boys, however variously those interests may be understood. In a sense the governors' concern with elementary education is the obverse of the practice of taking boarders into the houses of the Chief Master and Usher. They are both offshoots, in opposite directions, from the stem of the Charter's original intention – to teach Latin and Greek to Birmingham boys. One of these diverging branches sought to teach Birmingham boys subjects other than Latin and Greek, and the other to teach Latin and Greek to boys from outside Birmingham.

Perhaps a word should be said here about boarders. They appear to have been taken in the houses of the Chief Master and Usher from early in the school's history and there is nothing in the Charter to prohibit it. Such was common practice in the sixteenth century and onwards. But boarders paid. They paid because they did not live in the manor of Birmingham and so could not benefit from the free places which the original endowment existed to provide; for them, it was not a 'free' grammar school. This meant, of course, that boarders usually came from gentry, professional or clerical families. This was one of the submerged factors in the battles over the Charter in the 1680s. The kind of school

An easterly prospect of Birmingham, engraved for the Modern Universal British Traveller in 1779. The spire of St Martin's is on the left, the tower of St Philip's on the right and the Free Grammar School between.

that the citizens of Birmingham wanted was not necessarily the same as that which the gentry wanted. There had been occasions during the seventeenth century when it was felt that 'paying pupils' received more attention than 'day-boys' from the town because the former lived in close contact with the master.

However that may be, it was quite common in the seventeenth century for a schoolmaster known to be a successful teacher to be able to attract boys to his house from a considerable distance. Hough came to Birmingham from London to be taught by Brokesby. One of the points made against Billingsley in the early seventeenth century and against Parkinson in the early eighteenth century was that the numbers attracted to their houses as boarders fell. Billingsley could not seriously compete as a schoolmaster with the renowned Thomas Hall at the neighbouring grammar school at King's Norton and Parkinson's political views frightened boarders away. The school was both a day-school and a boarding-school and this fact was not irrelevant to the alignment of forces in the Charter battle of the 1680s. The final outcome of that episode was that control of the school reverted to and remained for a very long time with the town oligarchy, and this has meant, among other things, that the school has become exclusively a day-school. Had the Charter battle ended differently the school could well have followed the course of other historical grammar schools and become a boarding-school, attracting boys from no specific catchment area and from a rather different social background.

The development of these elementary schools shows the governors as sensitive to the educational needs of the town and so, perhaps, it is surprising that they do not seem to have been much involved in the considerable manufacturing and industrial expansion that was taking place in Birmingham. As a corporate body they were certainly affected by it. The sharp rise in land values which it brought in its wake and also land sales for canal building both brought substantial increases to the Foundation income. But manufacturers were not strongly represented on the governing body whereas the professional and merchant classes increasingly were. This was not so much that the governors were not sympathetic to manufacturing and industry but rather that the new captains of industry did not live at their works but moved out to nearby villages – Aston and King's Norton, for example – and so became automatically ineligible for election to the governing body. The Charter had stipulated that governors must be resident in the manor of Birmingham.

A further point was that the governors seem not to have been keen to recognise first-generation success. Sons of successful fathers apparently stood a better chance of being gathered to the bosom of the governing body than the fathers themselves. How else can we explain the failure of Matthew Boulton and James Watt, two particularly notable citizens of Birmingham, to become governors? Unless, perhaps, they felt that they had better things to do and did not see the Foundation as representing the spirit of nascent, industrial Birmingham. The scientific speculations of the Lunar Society may have been more to their taste. Whichever way it was, the fact suggests that Birmingham's most celebrated and inventive technological minds moved in circles that were different from those of the town's historical establishment, personified in the only corporate body that the town had as yet known – the governors of the Free Grammar School.

The above factors indicate something of the gap that was opening between the governors and the spirit of the new manufacturers of Birmingham. There is, however, a further point. As the century progressed the connection between the new industrialists and Dissent became closer. In the early years of the century, although the dissenting opinion had been more strongly represented on the governing body than solid Anglicanism, a fairly good balance had, on the whole, been maintained between the two. But by the second half of the century nonconformists nationally were becoming impatient of the patronising condescension that they sensed in the yearly indemnity granted to them to allow them to hold public office despite the Test and Corporation Acts. Hard-liners began to emerge demanding the repeal of those Acts and this, in its turn, provoked hard-liners on the establishment side who saw any attack on the ecclesiastical power of the Church of England as a threat to the State and to the monarchy. In this situation the governing body gradually lined up with the Established Church as, in a way, it had to; after all, it had been created by the head of that Church. From about 1770 the governors of the Free Grammar School had become a pronouncedly Anglican body with a preponderance of professional men and traders with, from the 1730s, a small sprinkling of clerics among them. This inevitably meant a coincidence of interest with the landed gentry and with the retail trade of the town; they all felt a threat from the powerful young giant growing up in their midst.

Such was the accumulation of causes behind the otherwise surprising fact that a body which had, at the start of the century, been decidedly Whig and Dissenting should, at the end of the century, have been Tory and Anglican. To such an extent was this the case that John Brook, the secretary to the governors, was prominent among the small group of influential citizens who directed the infamous Priestley riots of 1790. These riots attacked and destroyed the property of known Dissenters, starting with that of the Unitarian minister and scientist, Dr Joseph Priestley. By this time, of course, the whole national establishment had become alarmed by the French Revolution, and as the Revolution escalated into the Terror and then into war with England, so alarm escalated into panic, and the Church and State loyalites of the governing body became more inflexible and pronounced.

A contemporary print showing the Birmingham riots of 1790.

Yet, however the political affiliations of the governors may have developed in the last decades of the eighteenth century they continued to encourage a modest extension of the practical education that Birmingham required. Competition from private schools (particularly nonconformist ones) may have been an additional spur but the governors' policy to extend educational opportunities remains an undeniable fact. In 1773 the extended syllabus of reading, writing and casting accounts was offered to all boys in the English School and not merely twenty of them. By the end of the century all the external elementary schools were teaching these three subjects. The governors appointed teachers to teach evening schools, and at their meeting on 21 October 1794 ordered that 'a school be opened in some convenient part of the town for the education of forty girls, and that a proper governess be appointed to instruct them'. The following meeting named Mrs Tinton as the mistress and fixed her salary at £30 a year.

But when it came to expanding the syllabus of the grammar school the terms of the Charter enforced caution. Some geography seems to have found its way into the syllabus earlier in the century without anybody noticing and in 1773 the governors took a deep breath and decided to appoint a French master, though they were careful to restrict drastically the number of boys who could be exposed to contact with that dangerous language. At a meeting on 7 July 1773 they ordered that:

> A French master well qualified for the teaching and instructing the French language shall forthwith be enquired after and appointed . . . for the teaching and instructing of five of the scholars of the said school . . . and the said French master shall be . . . paid a salary of twenty pounds a year.

The experiment did not last long, however, for in 1779 Mr Wratislava, the master whom they had appointed, resigned. Yet twenty years later at their meeting on 19 January 1798 we find the governors resolving to meet the wishes of boys who wanted to learn French and to take lessons in drawing, and that 'the head master be requested to make an enquiry and inform the governors at the next meeting what number of boys are desirous to have the advantage of such additional instruction'. There was certainly novelty in the notion of finding out what the pupils (or their parents) actually wanted. Nevertheless, it is fairly clear that in the last years of the century the numbers seeking a classical education still remained viable. Evidence for this is that over the last half of the century the governors thought it worth while to use some of the Foundation's increased income to increase the number and value of school exhibitions to the universities. Their value was raised from £20 to £35. Early in the following century they were to reduce the number of years for which an exhibition could be held from seven to four, thereby increasing the number available. These steps may have encouraged a few university aspirants. It is worth noting, though, that well over 50 per cent of these exhibitions went to boarders from outside Birmingham rather than to boys from the town.

Presiding over the grammar school while these developments were taking place during the last three decades of the century were two amiable Chief Masters, perfectly good classical scholars but not striking personalities. The first was John Brailsford, on whom a splendid collection of the eighteenth-century's favourite epithets was bestowed when he died, a collection which is almost comprehensive. He was 'courteous, hospitable and compassionate, polite without arrogance and liberal without ostentation, a truly benevolent and good man'. Moreover, he carried out 'the sacred duties of his profession with a zeal and sincerity every way becoming a faithful servant of that Church of which he was a distinguished member'. His profession was, of course, that of clerk in holy orders rather than that of schoolmaster and we must note that, like Mainwaring and Wilkinson before him, he retained parochial duties outside Birmingham. Unlike Mainwaring, however, he was punctilious in paying a substitute to cover his teaching at school when he was not there. He remained Chief Master for ten years after Thomas Greene's death in 1766; perhaps for us the most remarkable

fact about him is that he is the first Chief Master of whom a portrait exists. It looks down benignly on those sixth-form boys who today sit on the right-hand side of Big School during school assemblies.

Brailsford's successor was Thomas Price. His term of office – 1776 to 1798 – was twice as long as Brailsford's and one at least of his pupils, H. F. Cary, has acquired an enduring national reputation. Cary was the first widely read translator of Dante, and he wrote of Price, 'His name I cannot mention without reverence and appreciation'. No teacher can ask for a more gratifying compliment. Cary also noted the difference between 'the care and attention his Birmingham schoolmasters had given him and the casual methods almost universal in Oxford colleges'. He was not the last pupil from the school to make this sobering discovery. An exact contemporary of Cary and so also a pupil of Price was Rann Kennedy who returned to the school to spend most of his life there as Usher. This in itself is not remarkable but the man himself was. He was one of the best classical scholars of his time, a man of letters and a friend of Coleridge, evidence in itself of real intellectual life. He was also a respected parish priest and described by Washington Irving as 'a most eccentric character ... a man of real genius ... one of the queerest mortals living'. He was remembered in 1901 as 'flying round his desk, cane in hand, endeavouring to thrash a boy who dodged in and out in his fruitless efforts to escape – this to the immense amusement of the otherwise grave Headmaster, to say nothing of our own'.

With the appointment of John Cooke as Chief Master in 1798 the list of eighteenth-century Chief Masters ends as it began, with a controversial figure.

Birmingham in 1795.

H. F. Cary (1772–1834), translator of Dante.

47

This seal seems to have disappeared during the Charter quarrels (see Appendix 1). It was subsequently discovered by accident at Leicester in 1801 and bought for two guineas.

When he was appointed he had already been Usher for five years and his appointment to the Chief Mastership was energetically contested. The contestant was George Croft, the curate of St Martin's, scourge of nonconformists and strong partisan of the Established Church. When Cooke was elected Croft claimed that the election was invalid because two of the governors who had voted for him were ineligible to be governors. His case was not, however, sustained and Cooke was duly confirmed in office. T. W. Hutton has called him 'an enigma', largely, one supposes, because his record furnishes us with contradictory evidence about his character and his Chief Mastership. It is certainly possible to sit beneath his portrait in Big School for nearly forty years and still to be uncertain of what to read in his face. Does it radiate gentle benignity or cold cruelty? The portrait was commissioned by his parishioners at St Bartholomew's and presented to the school to be hung in a prominent place. It is by some way the most interesting of the portraits of previous Chief Masters that today subject the boys sitting below them to admonitory scrutiny.

Cooke ruled for thirty-six years. In 1828, towards the end of his time as Chief Master, the report of the Commissioners for Inquiring concerning Charities appeared and it gives so informative a picture of the working of the school at the time that it is worth quoting at length:

> The instruction given in the grammar school is divided into four departments. The principal of these, consisting of the most advanced scholars, is under the teaching of the head-master, the Rev. J. Cooke. The second department consisting of boys one degree less advanced, is under the management of the Rev. Francis Freer Clay, the headmaster's assistant. The third, consisting of boys still less advanced, is under the management of the Rev. Rann Kennedy, the second master or usher: and the fourth, consisting of the younger boys, is under that of the Rev. John Darwell, the assistant to the second master. The first three of these masters occupy, for the purposes of instruction, different parts of the large schoolroom; the fourth teaches his scholars in another room, constituting the ground floor of one of the wings of the building. The children are admitted into the school upon the recommendation of a governor; and are placed, after being examined as to their proficiency, in that department of the school for which they appear to be fit, and they are passed from the lower to the upper departments in succession. The instruction given in Mr. Darwell's department is, the rudiments of Latin, construing, the writing of easy exercises. On Saturday the boys repeat the Church catechism, and read the prayers, with the epistles and gospels for the ensuing Sunday. In Mr. Kennedy's class the boys are carried on in Latin, and sometimes, but not always, enter upon the Greek grammar; Mr. Kennedy also instructs them in geography. Mr. Clay carries them still further in Latin and Greek; and instructs a few of them in geography once a week. Mr. Cooke completes their classical education; he further requires his scholars to read history and geography, and examines them as to their acquirements therein. The attendance of the masters, in all the grammar departments is from about half past seven till nine, and from ten till twelve, every morning; in the afternoon, they attend in the three upper departments, on Mondays, Wednesdays and Fridays from about half past two till five; and the master of the lower school attends on Thursdays and Fridays, from two till five. The writing master attends, in the apartments over Mr. Darwell's school, on Mondays, Wednesdays and Fridays from two till five o'clock, when the boys of Mr. Darwell's department are taught; and on Tuesdays and Thursdays from two till four, when the boys of the other departments are taught.

It is interesting to note that admission was still by the recommendation of a governor and that in the grammar school the classroom time adds up to twenty-five hours per week, slightly more than today. But, of course, the masters' work load was very much less. Each master taught only one class so there was very much less correction to be done, and even the most lively imagination cannot envisage Cooke and his colleagues tripping round a rugger pitch, or feeling that their duty required them to undertake the hundred and one tasks outside the classroom that are obligatory today.

A revealing light is thrown on the school in the last years of Cooke's Chief Mastership in a *Reminiscence* by the Revd. Samuel Ellis, published in the *OE Gazette* in December 1892. He gives details of the way in which Latin and Greek were taught. *The Eton Greek Grammar* which was in use in the school at the time was written in Latin, as were the notes to the Greek texts that were used. Though Greek composition was not practised 'much attention was paid to Latin composition, both in prose and verse'. He describes Cooke as 'an elegant Latin scholar and a good teacher' and records that in Cooke's final years he held his classes in his house. When Ellis was in the first class he had only one companion, William Linwood, who was to become the editor of *Aeschylus* and a very distinguished classical scholar indeed. Ellis concludes:

John Cooke, nicknamed 'Butcher', Chief Master (1797–1834).

> It will be observed that no mention had been made of school games; none in fact existed, though in the extreme lower end of the old premises there were two playgrounds intended for the boarders, but as they were very few in number, only two or three in each house, little use was made of them, except perhaps in the winter for snowballing. Nothing was heard, either in the School or in the town, of those at present exciting pastimes, cricket and football.

Since there seem to be two faces to Cooke we must confront both. During his Chief Mastership the number of boys in the school fell and there was finally only one boarder left in his house. Discipline degenerated and he is said to have told the bailiff that on occasion he had to call the police to restore order. We learn that both he and the Usher, Rann Kennedy, were often late in making an appearance and it would not be unnatural to suppose that this spread to the boys. But above all Cooke and his two principal assistants acquired a reputation for excessive corporal punishment, 'a trinity of fiends', as they have been picturesquely described. It was not for nothing that he was called 'Butcher' Cooke. Even parents who were quite ready to accept the principle that beating is an essential part of the educational process felt that Cooke rather overstepped the mark. When one of them wrote to suggest that his son might do better if encouraged rather than beaten Cooke returned a flattening answer. 'The purport of your letter to me', he wrote, 'is as frivolous as it is impertinent ... I assure you that no interference of yours will produce any change in my treatment of your boys ... But you have an easy remedy, and will best consult our mutual satisfaction by adopting it, in the removal of your sons to some master who will receive with deference your lessons on education, and treat them with the requisite indulgence.' One would have to look a long way today to find a headmaster who could write a sentence of such magisterial resonance.

The story of Cooke's Chief Mastership, however, is by no means all negative. Former pupils remembered him with affection and gratitude. One such, who had

The legendary Rann Kennedy in later life from an early Daguerreotype.

An attractive sketch of the Hen and Chickens, showing the Georgian school building on the right of the picture.

been a boarder in Cooke's house, was bold to say, 'I have received much kindness from him and the whole family'. When another pupil from the Cooke era, Robert Radford, later to become Rector of Lincoln College, Oxford, returned to the school as an examiner he refused payment for his services because he felt that he owed the school so much. Cooke was certainly a good teacher (when he turned up) as testified by the fact that several of his pupils, not least the classical scholar, Linwood, became very distinguished in their subsequent careers. Examiners who came to the school as late in Cooke's career as 1831 reported that the senior boys 'were distinguished by a variety of miscellaneous information as well as by minute grammatical skill, seldom surpassed in any establishment we have had the opportunity of witnessing'. A steady succession of exhibitioners to the universities was maintained. He also re-established French in the curriculum – for the third time of asking.

In fact, there was little enigma about Cooke. He was an able man, no worse than most of his predecessors and better than several, but he went on too long. The governors' meeting of 15 April 1833 heard a letter from him in which he wrote of being 'liable to a pulmonary complaint', which, he claims, is aggravated

50

'by an early exposure of myself to the morning air' and asks that he may postpone his 'attendance in the school until after breakfast'. This the governors granted but added sternly that 'it is expected that Mr. Cooke will receive his class at his own house before breakfast.' They added that 'their duty impels them to require on the part of the masters a more strict attendance at the appointed hours and a more vigilant attention to the general discipline of the school'. But living in a tied house and his pension dependent upon the governors' benevolence what else could he do? Like all his eighteenth-century predecessors, with the sole exception of Hausted, he continued in office until he dropped. (Interestingly, the record in the previous century and in the succeeding century is precisely the reverse; in each case only one Chief Master died in office, Thompson in the seventeenth century and Vardy in the nineteenth.) Not surprisingly Cooke became tired as well as unwell and the combination of maladies rendered him less than efficient. As for his propensity to use implements of chastisement, the belief that sound learning was most readily acquired through the backside had a long and very respectable pedigree. Dr Johnson is authoritative on the subject: 'My master whipt me very well. Without that, Sir, I should have done nothing.' His master, John Hunter, is thought to have taught at the Birmingham School before going to Solihull and thence to Lichfield. According to Johnson he used to say while flogging his boys, 'I do this to save you from the gallows'. As a matter of interest Johnson believed that beating was a less harmful motivator than the spirit of competition, for he went on to say, 'The rod produces an effect which terminates in itself ... whereas by exciting emulation and comparisons of superiority you lay the foundations of lasting mischief; you make brothers and sisters hate each other.' At any rate, wholesale beating at King Edward's School did not cease with Cooke's death, as the boys who sat at the feet of his successor found out soon enough.

Although all but two years of Cooke's long Chief Mastership (1798–1834) fell in the nineteenth century he was essentially an eighteenth-century figure. During that century the school had certainly not stagnated. A new building had been constructed and the library specially housed. The governors had acquired a permanent secretary and their administration had become much more efficient; they had also started to think about other matters than collecting rents, about their responsibilities to the education of Birmingham and to take steps accordingly. Towards the end of the century masters' salaries had risen considerably. In 1762, the year in which James Boswell set up in London as a man of pleasure on an allowance of £200 per year, the Chief Master of King Edward's School was earning a salary of £88.15s.0d. plus a house. At the end of the century that salary had risen to £200 a year plus house. If by the time of Cooke's death big changes were becoming imperative that does not diminish what had been achieved in the eighteenth century once the 'rank, stinking Whig' and the 'cut-throat' had passed from the scene.

Portrait-bust of David Cox, leading Birmingham artist of the nineteenth century and pupil at King Edward's School.

51

5

The New Broom

All changed, changed utterly:
A terrible beauty is born.

W. B. Yeats: *Easter 1916*

I can cope with a new broom but this is a bloody vacuum cleaner.

Anonymous Schoolmaster

Francis Jeune, Chief Master
(1834–38), from a painting
in Pembroke College, Oxford.

SUCH MAY HAVE been the sentiments of both teachers and pupils at the Free Grammar School in Birmingham in 1834 after a month or two of the new Chief Master, Francis Jeune. In August 1834, the month in which Jeune's appointment was confirmed, Mr Darwell, head of the English School, retired owing to ill-health, and in December of the same year (the year in which his old friend, Coleridge, died) Rann Kennedy asked for permission to do likewise. He had served the school for nearly forty years and he claimed that 'my power of attention [is] neither so pliable nor unwandering as it formerly was'. One knows the feeling. The governors granted him a pension of £150 a year and he retired as from 25 March 1835.

Dr Jeune, a former Fellow of Pembroke College, Oxford, and a native of the Channel Islands, was twenty-eight years old when he arrived in Birmingham. Although it goes without saying that he was a first-rate classical scholar his choice may occasion some surprise as he was a protégé of Lord John Russell, a fact calculated to send shivers down the Tory spines of the governors of the school. For Russell was a highly placed and effective Whig politician, closely associated with the 1832 Reform Bill and with the recent repeal of the Test and Corporation Acts which had smoothed the way to advancement for Dissenters; he also numbered among his ancestors one who had been executed under Charles II for treasonable republicanism. When we take account of these background facts it is much to the credit of the school governors that, in spite of his having so alarming a sponsor, they saw in Jeune the man for the task that they knew had to be done, to wit, the revitalising of the school after Cooke's lackadaisical

A slightly later sketch of the Hen and Chickens than that on page 50, showing the addition of an imposing portico.

final years in office. That task was not going to be made easier by the fact that the governors had just taken the decision to pull down the main school buildings in New Street and to build a magnificent new school. It is to this that we must turn our attention before considering both what Jeune achieved during his brief Chief Mastership and how he achieved it.

In April 1821 the governors had appointed a committee to report on the condition of the school building, then nearly a hundred years old. The survey was conducted by a reputable local architect, Thomas Rickman, and its conclusions were deeply depressing. Rickman had found that the school building was dangerously unsafe (all the roof-timbers needed renewing for a start) and that money spent on repairs would be money thrown away. He reported that 'patching done at once and at considerable expense would probably make the School safe to use for *at most* seven years' and furthermore that he considered 'the expense of a complete repair would be greater than that of erecting new buildings'. Either way large expenditure seemed unavoidable.

The severe shock of Rickman's report was not a single spy; battalions of other troubles were at hand. Where was the money to come from? Would the Lord Chancellor allow developments that extended beyond the provisions of the Charter? Would Parliament sanction the raising of necessary finance? What should be done about the Foundation elementary schools and the English School? Where should the new school (or schools) be sited? What would public opinion in the town have to say about the governors' use of their endowment? The necessity of a new building acted as a catalyst to bring all these problems into a single focus and to make radical change unavoidable. Moreover a new and worrying question emerged to keep the governors awake at night: in face of the rapidly growing civic consciousness of the town how far were they going to be able to keep the control of developments exclusively in their own hands?

As it happened, a month before they appointed the Rickman committee the governors had created a separate committee to report on 'the propriety of abolishing the small schools and establishing in their stead one school for boys and one for girls to be educated on the system of the National Society'. The motive had been the need to retrench which had been recognised even before the bombshell of Rickman's report. The prospect of reorganising the Foundation schools and now at the same time building a new one put the affairs of the whole Foundation into a condition of flux in which several considerations predominated. The two most important were the organisation of non-grammar school education within the Foundation and the siting of the new school and its satellites. Several ways of organising the education offered in the elementary/commercial/English school(s) were considered and it would be tedious to trace their permutations, but the important fact is that the town now considered that it was involved and that its wishes should be taken into account. As for the question of siting, it was tempting to consider using the New Street site to house an enlarged English School which would provide a commercial curriculum and to resite the grammar school outside the town, a course which, as it happened, the Lord Chancellor had approved. This plan, however, did not suit public opinion in Birmingham. Perhaps we can form the clearest picture of a confused situation if we look at the objections which inhabitants of the town raised against a Bill which the governors were seeking to have passed in Parliament. This Bill, the Birmingham Free Grammar School Bill, embodied the governors' proposals for solving the Foundation's problems. The petitioners to the House of Commons objected that the Bill would:

(i) remove the classical school from its present central situation ... where it is accessible ... to one of the vicinities of the town, where it will be accessible to but few of the inhabitants;

(ii) postpone the erection of the commercial school ... until the completion of the classical school and the happening of certain remote and doubtful contingencies;

(iii) despoil the inhabitants of one school whilst it is very doubtful whether they would ever obtain the other;

(iv) make no provision out of the ample funds of the charity for the elementary instruction of the poorer classes;

(v) not propose to improve the government of the school, or to secure greater activity and responsibility for the future, notwithstanding the charity commissioners have in their report animadverted most severely upon the conduct of the governors, and pointed out several instances of flagrant mismanagement on their part.

The first four of these objections obviously bear upon the considerations under discussion. The fifth raises another matter altogether, one which was to haunt the governing body for fifty years because what it finally boiled down to was a pronounced scepticism as to the competence of a self-electing oligarchy. It opposed the fact that the governors should be an entirely co-opted body and implied the dreaded possibility of governors nominated by outside bodies, worst of all by the town council. After much debate, many hearings and what the governors could have regarded as betrayal by Lord Chancellor Brougham, a compromise was achieved. The Classical School and masters' houses were to be built on an extended New Street site, boarders were to be allowed but their numbers tightly controlled, a Commercial School to be built on an adjacent site and begun in 1833, and four elementary schools to be maintained in different parts of the town. The governors had successfully resisted attempts to alter their own mode of election but had thought it best to drop a clause that would have prevented Dissenters from being eligible. This did not mean that they actually had to elect any of them.

With the ground thus cleared it was possible to invite architects to submit designs for the new Classical School. The successful competitor was Charles Barry who was later to win national fame by designing the Houses of Parliament. Barry was often less than precise about expenditure and his estimates of costs caused the governors many a headache as they were so often underestimates. The Act of Parliament sanctioned borrowing up to £30,000 and after suitable adjustments to his design Barry was able to claim that his scheme would remain within that limit. But in their maddening way costs escalated. The governors themselves insisted on Darley Stone because the Birmingham atmosphere necessitated stone that would weather well, labour costs rose as a result of primitive trade-union activity, one contractor resigned and the next died before the building was finished, and costly precautions against dry-rot were thought advisable. All this meant that the original estimate was considerably exceeded and permission to borrow again had to be sought. But the resulting building was, in the words of Francis Goodwin, Barry's final rival for the commission, 'not merely an ornament to Birmingham but to England'.

Barry's building stood until 1936 and so for almost exactly a century it was a major architectural feature in the town. It is certainly a potent fact in many a living Edwardian's memory of his schooldays. Whether or not it exerted the deep spiritual influence upon its inmates that T. W. Hutton claimed for it is

Barry's building in New Street.

The Upper Corridor in New Street. The centre door led into Big School and the top of the Boys' Staircase can be seen at the end of the corridor on the left. This corridor was rebuilt on the new site at Edgbaston and since 1953 has been the school's chapel.

difficult to determine. Not all schoolboys are susceptible to spiritual influences. But that it was a fine building, one of the two or three finest in the Birmingham of its time, is beyond dispute. Bearing its date of design in mind one is not surprised that Barry chose the Gothic style for this large and important public building. It was one of the earliest and most successful examples of Victorian Gothic, designed by a very talented architect before the style declined into the portentous cliché that it all too often became later in the century. His design had the vitality of a new style, and in that style Barry achieved a more satisfyingly harmonious building than did Hansom and Welch in the hybrid classicism of Birmingham Town Hall, built in the same decade.

The overall design envisaged a rectangular structure containing within itself two courtyards. Each end of the building was conceived as a separate house, one for the Chief Master and one for the Second Master plus their respective boarders, though with the passage of time both of these houses were taken over as classrooms and the masters went to live elsewhere. The Gothicising of Barry's building was thoroughgoing. Externally there were buttresses, battlements, finials, crockets, large windows each with three trefoil-headed lights. Internally the corridors were reminiscent of cathedral architecture and the furnishings, thought to have been designed by Pugin who was working at the time with Barry, were conceived accordingly. Barry wisely located most of the business part of the school on the first floor in order to ensure light in the event of his school being surrounded by other tall buildings and to avoid the dust and smells of the street. Gas lighting was installed, a very up-to-date amenity. The most imposing feature of the whole building, however, was the room marked on the plan as Grammar School and actually known as Big School. At one end of this lofty hall the Chief Master taught from a large, imposing wooden structure that combined desk, throne and canopy, designed by Pugin and bearing across the front of the canopy, the stark proclamation – *Sapientia*. This magnificent object, redolent of authority both regal and episcopal, is still in daily use, and the present writer, who for many years had to supervise its removal every time he wanted to direct a play rehearsal, can testify that its weight required the brawn of several hefty actors to move it, even though it ran on castors.

Enthroned in *Sapientia* and surrounded on three sides by the disciples at their feet, the great Victorian Chief Masters dispensed godliness and good learning if not always sweetness and light. From a similar but more modest desk at the other end of the room, 102 feet away, the second master did the same, and later four further teaching positions, two on each side, were created down the sides of the hall, each with its desk and overhead sounding-board. There was no place here for the languid young man who was watching his eyelashes grow a hundred years before in the Georgian building. The almost domestic scale of that building, which could have been a gentleman's house, had given place to a building which was deliberately impressive and which, although the result of private enterprise, expressed something of the way the town was increasingly coming to think of itself; it was thinking big. Barry's triumph was to create a building that satisfied these civic aspirations with considerable refinement yet without the pomposity that they often engender. The town might well have been grateful to the school governors who had been the 'onlie begetters' of one of its most distinguished ornaments.

This fine building came into use in January 1838. By that time Jeune had been Chief Master for three and a half years and all of that time he had been running a school that had operated in one large and three small rooms in the Shakespeare Theatre in New Street. From the start he was a man with a mission and not one to waste time. The governors' meeting on 30 April 1834, immediately following Cooke's death, had appointed a committee to report to them 'the fresh statutes to be made touching the future order, government and direction of the headmaster and usher and assistant masters'. This sounds as if the governors were intent on tightening their control of the masters, and this bracing desire for discipline was soon extended to the boys. The agent of this extension was the Chief Master. We are indebted to T. W. Hutton for preserving for us two splendid examples of Jeune's direct approach to the task of raising standards. The first is a reminiscence, made at a School Dinner in 1903, by Lt.-Col. S. D. Williams, sixty-seven years after leaving school in 1836. He recalled that:

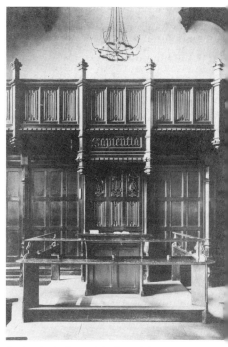

Sapientia in its original position in Barry's Big School.

> Jeune said he would insist on punctuality, threatening us with one cut for each minute late. We scoffed at the idea; we had survived dire threats even from the governors. I turned up, as usual, a quarter of an hour late, and was slinking quietly to my place when I met Jeune. He merely looked up at the clock and told me to hold out my hand. I got fifteen cuts and was never late again.

His second example was from the diary of Sir Francis Galton, one of the school's most distinguished pupils:

1836

Jan. 25	Black Monday, return to school. The Doctor flogged a chap. The Dr.'s father was buried.
Mar. 15	One boy expelled, another flogged.
Mar. 17	D____ expelled.
Mar. 26	Got caned.
Mar. 28	Got caned.
April 1	Good Friday, we were made to fast but we went over to the grub shop and got plenty.
April 2	The Doctor did not go round with his cane.

But so far, Jeune was only limbering up. He must then have gone into hard training for by autumn Galton was writing to his sister:

Oct. 27	I have not been able to write on account of the hard work and the many impositions I have lately had – 30 one day and 10 pages of Greek Grammar to write out, 40 next day and 40 next. Another boy has left. Indeed I have never known such an unhappy and unlucky school as this; 2 more will leave at Christmas, and I would give anything if I could leave too ... I do not like the Doctor taking our class, he expects the grammar said more perfectly than we can and he thrashes the lower part of the body for every mistake they make in construing; this morning he thrashed eleven fellows in 8 minutes.

There is no doubt that Jeune was an intimidating character. The Revd C. P. Male, an old boy who later became a master at the school, recalled that Jeune 'had but little of the *suaviter in modo*, with a superabundance of the *fortiter in re*'. He added that 'his countenance was enough to inspire any schoolboy with awe'

Big School in New Street. Note the gallery at the far end with *Sapientia* below. School honours boards are on the right-hand wall.

and that 'his method did not lead me to take interest in, still less to love, the works which I read'. Furthermore 'his [Jeune's] plodding on with a Greek Testament lesson on a Sunday afternoon in 1835 while a total solar eclipse was proceeding, with a cloudless sky, and lighting the gas as darkness drew on, was to me an unpardonable offence.' But Male also tells a humanising story of Jeune jumping with fright at a rat in the classroom and then relating that as a boy he had been seized by the throat by a rat.

An intriguing reminiscence by Charles Evans, later to become Chief Master of the school, describes his first day at King Edward's. He arrived in January 1838, just as the school moved into Barry's new building. He records his awe at the conversation of a couple of slightly older boys engaged in 'a somewhat profound discussion on foreknowledge and free will', and also that 'another boy, Francis Galton, argued that it was a waste of time for him to write Latin verses and learn Ovid repetition, and that we all ought to study Mechanics and Natural Science, for he had just seen a splendid engine, by Sharp and Roberts, at Vauxhall station, and neither Virgil nor Homer could have made that.' He also gives us a charming vignette of life in Big School on that first morning of its use in which unsuspected shortcomings are immediately apparent and the formidable Dr Jeune appears in more genial light.

In the course of the morning as we stood round the Head Master's desk, a loud volume of sound reached us from the lower end of the room, with piercing cries of 'SILENCE'; come here, that boy who is talking yonder, come here.' Whereupon some six little boys standing up to obey the summons – 'No, no, no, that boy there who was talking, come here sir: you know very well who I mean.' Some three other

The cloisters in the central quadrangle of Barry's building.

boys then rising from their seats – 'NO, NO, NO,' cried the Second Master, 'Not you: go back – that other boy come here sir. No, no, not you! you, sir, come here.'

'I am afraid,' said the Head Master, 'that the Architect does not understand acoustics: there seems to be a great echo in the room: or is it possible that I make such a noise as that? Do I really?'

In the afternoon 'ambrosial cakes and decanters of nectar' were produced and in came two governors and the architect and the new school was declared to be open and there were prayers and speeches and 'we were all told to write a copy of elegiacs on "a goose quill" and to learn by heart eight lines of Ovid'.

Inducing the habit of work was not, however, Jeune's only achievement. In 1836, after two years at the school, he had written to the governors a letter of the greatest importance. It is a splendid piece of writing, a model of expository prose, not least, perhaps, because he was innocent of legal training. He surveyed the situation in which the school found itself, isolated the main problems and proposed a solution. The problems had not gone unperceived in the past nor had the solution been unscouted, but it was the clarity and force of Jeune's analysis that concentrated the governors' minds to the point where they could see that what he proposed was irresistible. In this case, there really was 'no other way'.

He begins by pointing out that the 'magnificent edifice' that the governors had just had built would be wasted if it were to house only the Classical School. Such expense for the benefit of only 150 boys would not be good sense. The school must cater for 'the wants of a great commercial community'. He asserts (rather defensively) the superiority of a classical education but adds 'I do not think it impossible to devote some portion of time to modern languages and the mathematical and scientific pursuits without endangering the great and primary object of our institution'. He makes the case for a balanced education for all, even those who aim at the universities and so will specialise in classics. He then changes to what must have been a very persuasive economic argument, to wit, that if the Classical and Modern Schools function in one building there will be no need to build another which, considering the escalated costs of Barry's building, was no small consideration. He points out further that the existence of two separate schools, one of them housed in a building of notable splendour and the other not, will create bad feeling and a situation which 'party animosity' will not fail to exploit. If a second school were to be built it would not be completed for several years and therefore for those years the town would lose the benefit of a large number of places. Such were the arguments for joining the Classical and Modern Schools in one building and for a broader curriculum for all boys.

The rest of Jeune's letter is taken up with details of how the school could be organised if his main contention is accepted, details of curriculum and of staffing. He envisages a considerable expansion of staff, putting the teachers of non-classical subjects on the same footing as the others and the use of occasional outside lecturers. He makes the revolutionary claim that English authors should be studied 'with the same accuracy, analysed with the same rigour, committed to memory and imitated in daily composition' as classical authors. Not all of that prescription had actually sunk in a hundred years later. Jeune was not enthusiastic for the elementary schools as he thought that church schools were doing that job

The Hen and Chickens building photographed with the corner of Barry's school just visible in the right of the picture.

quite well enough. He suggested instead schools for 'a sound but plain commercial education'. His last point shows that he well understood the real nature of the problem that Cooke's final years had exposed. He urged that the governors should be empowered to give a pension to those whom he described as 'superannuated assistants'.

Most of Jeune's suggestions were acted upon in due course. It can even be said that his recommendation about changing the nature of the elementary schools, though dropped at the time, bore fruit fifty years later in the creation of the Foundation grammar schools. It is clear that administration was his strong suit and he was the first Chief Master since Brokesby to have creatively affected the development of the Foundation. Those in between had left development to the governors. Having now, as he saw it, sorted out Foundation affairs, put the school on the right course for the future and seen it established in what he referred to as its 'noble halls', Jeune accepted the offer of the Deanery of Jersey. He swept off to the Channel Isles, then to the mastership of his old college and finally to the bishopric of Peterborough. But the mark of his four years at King Edward's School has been indelible.

6

Chief Master as Guru

Well had the boding tremblers learned to trace
The day's disasters in his morning face;
. . . .
Yet he was kind, or if severe in aught,
The love he bore to learning was in fault.

Goldsmith: *The Deserted Village*

THE SCHOOL TODAY undoubtedly has behind it a long record of outstanding academic achievement. This has not come without energy and endeavour of a kind unknown in the centuries so far considered. That such a tradition has been built up is due in no small part to the ten-year Chief Mastership of Jeune's successor, James Prince Lee. He arrived at King Edward's School at a time when schools were beginning to be dimly aware of shock waves that had been rippling through the system for the past decade. These tremors were becoming too strong to be ignored and the new Chief Master came straight from their epicentre not far from Birmingham, to wit, from Rugby School, where since 1828 Dr Thomas Arnold had been injecting earnestness, both moral and intellectual, into the notion of education. Godliness and good learning fused in a single incarnation; schoolmaster became guru, the venerable teacher of the profoundest knowledge. It was in such a role that, between 1838 and 1848, Prince Lee transformed King Edward's School.

Prince Lee came to King Edward's School propelled by 'golden opinions from all sorts of people'. He had been head boy at St Paul's School, Craven Scholar at Trinity College, Cambridge, and then a Fellow of the college. One of his pupils there wrote that he was 'considered the finest classical tutor in the college'; and when he applied for the Chief Mastership of King Edward's School the Master of Trinity (where the most formidable of all classical scholars, the legendary Bentley, had also been master) wrote that he was:

generally considered one of the most distinguished classical scholars ever known in the university; and as a private tutor he was equally remarkable for the great range of his knowledge, for his clearness and precision in teaching, and for the deep and active interest which he always took in the welfare and success of his pupils.

That these admirable gifts were equally effective when applied to school-teaching Arnold's testimonial from Rugby, where Lee had taught for eight years, made clear. Arnold reinforced the points made by the Master of Trinity and testified further to Lee's popularity, his activity, his gentlemanliness, his religious zeal and his experience as a schoolmaster. According to the governors' minutes they were unanimous in their choice of Lee over the other two short-listed candidates for the Chief Mastership, but Male records that his election was secured by a majority of one vote as 'my father, Dr. Male, was somewhat too zealous in introducing him personally to several of the Governors, all of whom, as we understand, not fancying his appearance – a striking contrast to that of his predecessor – voted against him'.

In the *OE Gazette* of July 1891, Howard Pearson recalled his initial meeting with Lee forty-four years earlier when his mother took him to the school to be interviewed as a prospective scholar. Lee was, he remembered, 'swarthy, hirsute, and black of hair, lofty and condescending, clothed in the majesty of his gown'. He asked Mrs Pearson if she had taught her son any Greek or Latin. She said she had not. 'That is well', replied Lee, 'because when ladies have done so we always find that we not only have to teach their boys Greek and Latin, but also to unteach them all they have learned.'

When Lee arrived at King Edward's School he was faced with a great opportunity and a great challenge. He had to forge one school out of what had formerly been two separate schools functioning in two separate buildings, the Classical School and the English School. Henceforward they were to coexist in Barry's fine new building and it was up to Lee to see that the arrangement was successful. He had much going for him – the new building itself, his own remarkable pedagogical gifts and, in Sydney Gedge, an effective and loyal Second Master who knew the school. Pearson, who knew Gedge towards the end of his career, describes him as 'a man whose severities were wont to raise very ireful feelings – but they were very transitory, and we all, I think, loved him. It was not respect (we habitually called him "old Gedge"). It was affection. He was emphatically a straight man.' So determined was he to be straight that his own sons in the school had a pretty hard time of it at his hands.

Lee set quickly to work and at the end of his first year as Chief Master he could report that the monthly examinations that he had instituted had done much to improve performance; not only were they 'a stimulus to exertion ... to the boys' but equally a stimulus 'to watchfulness' in the masters. He also found they were a useful way of getting to know the boys. Examining the whole school himself and inspecting and examining the Foundation elementary schools was an important part of the Chief Master's job. In addition to this, the Classical School and the upper classes of the English School were examined each June by three external examiners, two appointed by the governors and one by the Chief Master. Fifty years after the event the Rev. Arthur Mozley recalled his two years as a very junior master in Lee's time and asserted that 'the great event of school life was then, as now, the annual examination. It was not a Government

James Prince Lee, Chief Master
(1838–48).

Inspector who came for this occasion, but one chosen by the governors of the school – i.e. the headmaster – for this important work.'

Initially, however, Lee's biggest task was to impose discipline on the large number of new boys. Many of these were boys of a type that had not previously been to the school and had been attracted as a result of Jeune's reforms. The diary of a boarder in Lee's house reveals that the windows in Big School were frequently broken as a result of rounders being played in that august chamber. Replacement costs varied between a shilling and half a crown. He finally wrote, 'I determine to play rounders no more. I broke three panes in the school today – 7s. 6d.' The boys were often involved in massed street battles against other boys in the town, battles in which they did not always come off second best. The artist, Sir Edward Burne Jones, who was at the school during the 1840s, recollected fifty years later that, 'I was stabbed at school ... in the groin. It didn't hurt much ... It was during prayers and so was kept from the headmaster of course.' So it is hardly surprising that when, during Lee's Chief Mastership, Anthony Trollope's brother, Thomas, taught briefly at the school he reported that he found himself 'a policeman among these turbulent lads'. Mozley, on the other hand, who was in charge of 'ninety boys, divided into three classes' records that he 'generally felt very happy among them, and had boys whom it was a pleasure to teach; or who, on the other hand, were an amusement from their inability to learn'. Lee comments on the tone of the school in the report to the governors mentioned above, and it is characteristic of his whole way of thinking that he should single out the moral shortcoming of lying rather than the social unacceptability of rowdyism:

> The moral state of the School I am happy to add is improved. Falsehood which at one time prevailed to a great extent, has much diminished. The number of boys punished severely for serious offences amounted in the first half year 1839 to 30. In the second half year it was reduced to 19. Of the latter, one was publicly expelled and eight others compelled to be privately withdrawn. This severity will not seem extravagant when the great difficulty is taken into consideration of reducing into discipline upwards of 200 boys many of them unused to all restraint, taken at once into a newly opened school where there was no routine established for them to fall into, as was the case in the important experiment of opening the new Department in 1838.

Clearly Lee did not undertake this task in kid gloves. Fifty years on, a disgruntled elderly Old Edwardian recalled in a letter to the *Birmingham Daily Mail* that Lee had given him a cut with the cane for being late. He added, with disarming candour, 'for years it rankled in my mind, and how I longed to punch that Bishop's head! But I never had the opportunity.' However, after five years at the school Lee could write in a summary of developments during his time at the school:

> In July 1838, on my election to the headmastership I found the Classical School then containing about 220 boys (now 235, its number as limited) and two elementary schools just opened, one for boys and one for girls, containing about 136 each. In 1839 I opened the English School with 215 boys, and in the same year two additional elementary schools for boys, holding together about 350, and one for 136 girls, were commenced. The whole seven schools are wholly under my superintendance ... In the elementary schools, besides religious instruction, the children are educated to qualify themselves for business. In the English School are taught, in addition to grammar, geography and history, French, drawing and the elements of mathematics, with the rudiments of Latin. In the Classical School the usual course of classical education in a public school is pursued, in preparation for the universities, with French, drawing and mathematics.

When the curricula of the Classical School and English School are put together we can see something like a familiar twentieth-century curriculum beginning to emerge. In many respects, however, Lee was a man of his times, revealed *in the way* he expresses in an examination report the idea, reasonable enough in itself, that some boys in the English School are not suited to its curriculum: 'Many of them are from habits, station in life and prospects, much more suited to one of the Elementary Schools than to the English School.' Social mobility, it would seem, was not a concept that came readily to his mind.

Another matter which engaged Lee's attention was the religious education offered in the school. The situation in King Edward's School differed markedly from that obtaining in the educational establishments that Lee had previously been connected with. A significant number of boys in the school came from Dissenting families who felt that the quality of education offered at King Edward's School made it worth while to risk contamination from so professedly Anglican an institution. In a letter to Sir James Pakington written in April 1843 Lee explained his policy regarding religious education. All pupils are required to attend school prayers but children from Dissenting families do not have to join in. Religious instruction is always first lesson of the day and Dissenters may absent themselves, having first produced a written request to do so. They may then come to school an hour later. Jewish pupils were allowed to come late on a Saturday and, once arrived, to do no written work, and Roman Catholics were allowed to be absent on feasts of obligation. Baptists were not to be asked questions which would offend them when being taught the Church Catechism and the boys' schools were to be open on Sunday for boys whose parents wished them to attend. Lee adds that there have been no complaints from Dissenters. His letter also contains the following interesting statistic breaking down the total number of boys in the school into their various religious denominations:

	Feb.1842	Mar.1843
Church of England	748	798
Independents	133	107
Wesleyans	116	122
Baptists	60	72
Socinians	38	30
Lady Huntingdon's Chapel	10	8
Roman Catholics	8	4
Swedenborgians	7	6
Presbyterians	6	8
Jews	4	4
Quakers	1	1
Calvinist	0	1
Irvingite	1	0
Plymouth Brethren	1	0
Total	1133	1161
Dissenters	385	363

It can be seen that Dissenters make up roughly a third of the total number of boys in the school but this bears little relation to the ratio between Anglicans and Dissenters in the town where Dissenters predominated. In these figures one can see the source of so much of the tension that existed between the school and the town council.

Lee's claim to be a great headmaster, however, rests principally on the enormous impact which his teaching and personality made on the boys whom he personally taught in the first class of the Classical School. It was not only that the academic results that his pupils subsequently achieved at Cambridge were by any standards remarkable, but the fact that they were marked for life by his personality, a compelling combination of rigorous intellect, range of knowledge, and high-minded concern with the serious business of existence. A further statistic tabulating the achievements of his pupils at Cambridge may be illuminating:

First Class in the Classical Tripos

1844	Henry Keary, Trinity	3rd aeq.
1845	Hubert Ashton Holden, Trinity	Senior aeq.
1845	Frederick Rendall, Trinity	Senior aeq.
1845	Thomas Cox, St John's	5th.
1847	Charles Evans, Trinity	Senior aeq.

Sir Francis Galton (1822–1911).

1847	John Smythe Purton, St Catherine's	8th.
1848	Brooke Foss Westcott, Trinity	Senior aeq.
1850	Henry Chance, Trinity	16th.
1851	Joseph Barber Lightfoot, Trinity	Senior.
1851	Christopher Blick Hutchinson, St John's	6th.
1852	Edward White Benson, Trinity	8th.
1852	James Thomas Pearce, Trinity	9th aeq.
1852	Arthur Ayres Ellis, Trinity	9th aeq.

In addition to these impressive Tripos results the same thirteen men collected sixteen assorted classical medals and scholarships and eight college fellowships. There were also nearly a dozen distinguished performances at Oxford but without the glitter of the ones at Cambridge. Subsequently, both Westcott and Lightfoot held the chair of Divinity at Cambridge and each became Bishop of Durham, Lightfoot first, Westcott second, Benson became headmaster of Wellington, Bishop of Truro and Archbishop of Canterbury, Purton became president of his college and Evans came back to King Edward's as Chief Master after Benson had been offered the job and decided otherwise. Even allowing for the fact that they were obviously a very talented group and would have done well whoever taught them, there is a consistency of achievement that suggests first-class teaching. Like all really good teachers Lee was a great encourager. Male, who as Lee quickly recognised had been 'cowed' by Jeune, attributed 'Lee's marvellous success as a teacher not more to his accurate scholarship and vast power of imparting it to others than to his knack of inspiring his pupils with confidence in him and in themselves'. He also recognised the importance of building up the confidence of junior masters. Mozley records, 'he gave the masters of the English School an occasional opportunity of being connected educationally with his first class. I remember once he sent this distinguished class to construe Horace before me; and Evans only last autumn reminded me . . . that I specially commended himself and Westcott as worthy of a first class at Oxford from their manner of translation.' Perhaps one ought here to observe that if Lee justly takes a good deal of credit for his brilliant pupils St Paul's can with the same justice take credit for him. Particularly illuminating with regard to Lee's teaching even if not strictly impartial is the testimony of its recipients. Lightfoot, Westcott and Benson have all left accounts of being taught by 'Mr. Lee', as they referred to him in their private correspondence. Westcott wrote:

> I can recall, as it were from a lesson of yesterday, the richness and force of the illustrations by which he brought home to us a battle piece of Thucydides, a landscape of Virgil, or a sketch of Tacitus; the eloquence with which he discoursed on problems of life and thought suggested by some favourite passage of Butler's *Analogy*; the depths which he opened to us in the inexhaustible fulness of the Apostolic words; the appeals which he made to our higher instincts, revealing us to ourselves, in the crises of our school history or in the history of the nation . . . He claimed us from the first as his fellow workers. He made us feel that in all learning we must be active and not receptive only . . . He encouraged us to collect, to examine, to arrange facts . . . we gained little by little a direct acquaintance with the instruments and methods of criticism, and came to know something of confident delight in using them.

Lee was a man of strong views, particularly on religious questions, a determined opponent of the Tractarian movement though without Charles Kingsley's loony obsession with its supposed unmanliness. It was what he regarded as its 'sacerdotalism' that aroused his hostility, as it did that of his sovereign who even regarded mid-week communion as evidence of that dangerous condition. Yet he was the last person to try to foist his personal views on his pupils. Rather than inculcate views he sought to develop in them a cast of mind which was insatiably curious, relentlessly accurate and very serious. One cannot quite see him placing 'intellectual ability' third in his list of priorities as Arnold had done. But there is no doubt that for the boys in the First Class he was literally their 'guru' — a venerated teacher whose teaching and example provided a never-forgotten lesson in the important subject of how to live. Lightfoot remembered a lesson on Butler's *Analogy* when he was in the First Class:

> Leaning back in his chair and folding his gown about him, he would break off at some idea suggested by the text, and pour forth an uninterrupted flow of eloquence for ½ an hour or more, the thought keeping pace with the expression all the while, and the whole marked by a sustained elevation of tone which entranced even the idlest and most careless among us.

Dr Lightfoot, Bishop of Durham (1879 – 89).

However, the lofty and self-confident certainty and the seemingly limitless resources of knowledge which made him so inspiring a teacher did not always commend him to adults who do not always appreciate being lectured to. To them his manner appeared autocratic (which it was) and arrogant (which it may or may not have been). Such a manner is an affliction to which many eminent men are prone and Lee was no exception. Yet Mozley shows us another side to Lee's character when he describes him as 'a pleasant, light-hearted man to talk to', and goes on to relate the incident in which Lee had found out that Mozley was going to the Wolverhampton races and came himself to tell him, with a wicked smile, that his horse had been brought round for him. He also puts it on record how kind and considerate to him Lee had been when he first arrived at the school straight from Oxford with only a pass degree.

Even if Lee seemed 'lofty and condescending' to the world at large it does not begin to account for the almost pathological campaign of vilification waged against him by a local surgeon, appropriately named Gutteridge. He had, however, impressed the Prince Consort on the latter's visit to Birmingham in 1843, and although not made tutor to the Prince of Wales, as at one time appeared likely, he was offered and accepted the appointment as first Bishop of Manchester. His star pupils were delighted that he should be thus honoured but the move was not a happy one; he exchanged the satisfactions of success and acclaim as a great and inspiring teacher for the gloomy disappointments of an increasingly uncongenial episcopate.

An alternative likeness of James Prince Lee, Chief Master (1838 – 48). It is difficult to see from this drawing why his appearance discommended him in the eyes of some governors.

When Lee left Birmingham in 1848 he had, through no fault of his own, become something of a controversial figure in the town. Within the school, however, his achievements had been so impressive that any successor was going to face a hard task in maintaining them. That successor was Edwin Hamilton Gifford who came from being an assistant master at Shrewsbury School and was, indeed, an Old Salopian. It may be worth noting at this point a connection between the two schools. In 1818 Rann Kennedy's eldest son, Benjamin Hall

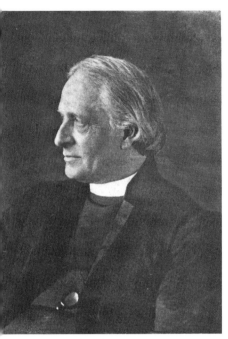

Edward White Benson,
Archbishop of Canterbury
(1883–96).

Kennedy, had been transferred from King Edward's School, where his father was Usher, to Shrewsbury School. After Cambridge he had returned to Shrewsbury and then succeeded to the headmastership in 1836. Like all Rann Kennedy's four sons he had won the Porson Prize at Cambridge and in company with two of his brothers had been Senior Classic. More to the immediate point, he would have taught Gifford in the latter's schooldays so it is perhaps not surprising that Gifford, too, became Senior Classic in his turn and a wrangler to boot, just at the time when the top classical honours at Cambridge were beginning to become the monopoly of Lee's pupils. When Gifford arrived to take up the Chief Mastership of King Edward's School he was, like Jeune fourteen years earlier, just twenty-eight.

Gifford, one suspects, was not without ambition because within two years of his arrival he was asking the governors to support his application for the headmastership of Rugby School, assuring them at the same time that if he should be unsuccessful they could continue to rely on his devotion to King Edward's. One senses a slight embarrassment in the elaborate phraseology of his letter. In spite of the splendid testimonial that the governors gave him he did not get the job and settled down to a further twelve years in Birmingham.

In 1852 the school celebrated its tercentenary. The opportunities for pomp and circumstance which academic and civic institutions seldom neglect were fully exploited. Aris's *Birmingham Gazette* records that:

> It seemed odd to witness the collegiate and academical robes, the lawn sleeves, the grave professors in their gowns, which one would expect to meet only in the cloisters of some old cathedral town, or in some out-of-the-way nook of a university, in the busy streets, and retiring learning and divinity elbowing commerce and bustling trade, in the very heart of manufacturing industry.

In spite of the picturesque, Charles Lambish style the writer has put his finger on the situation that has always given King Edward's School its distinctive character, the mingling of academia and manufacture. He describes the procession that prompted the above reflection:

> The children to the number of nearly 1400, formed into line, and ... walked in procession in the following order to St. Martin's Church: Two Beadles; Assistant Mistresses; The girls of the different schools, three abreast; The Mistresses; The boys of the elementary schools; The Masters; The English School; The Two Writing Masters; The classes, in order, three abreast, beginning with the lowest; Each Master following his classes; The Classical School; The French and German Master; The classes, in order, three boys abreast, beginning with the lowest class, each master following his own class; The old Pupils, not members of the universities; The Old Pupils, members of the universities, in academical dress; The former Master of the school (Prince Lee); Members of other schools; The Officers of the Queen's College; Dissenting Ministers; The Clergy; The Clerk of the Peace and Town Clerk; The Aldermen; The Borough Magistrates; M.P.s for the Borough and County; The Archdeacon of Coventry, Dr. Jeune, and the Chancellor of the Diocese; The Mayor and the Recorder; The Bishop of Worcester, The Bishop of Manchester; The Bishop's Chaplains; Architect, Counsel and Solicitor; General Visitors; Peers of the Realm; Former Governors, Governors; Secretary.

The attentive reader may have noticed one or two surprising features in the above account. The first is that there are two simultaneous manifestations of Lee in the same procession, once as 'the former Master' and once as the Bishop of Manchester; the second is that Gifford does not appear at all, unless he is marching in modest anonymity behind his class among boys from the Classical School. We are told further that when everyone was safely stowed in St Martin's Church they listened to prayers read by the rector, the lessons by Gifford, the litany by Lee and a sermon by Jeune on the stirring theme that 'intellectual cultivation had always accompanied the gospel when preached in its fulness'. That final qualifying clause carefully guards against any dangerous flirting with Tractarian mediaevalism. The sermon itself was an exposition, in a tone that did not brook contradication, of standard Broad Church ideas, culminating in a meditation, *pour encourager les autres*, on the sad, early death of Henry Keary, one of Lee's brilliant pupils.

It was in the middle of Gifford's Chief Mastership, in November 1856 to be exact, that a magazine appeared which called itself *King Edward the Sixth's Monthly Magazine*. It was not the first attempt at a school magazine as fifteen years earlier, in 1842, the *King Edward the Sixth's Magazine* had appeared. This seems to have been largely the brainchild of Westcott and its editorial announced, rather dauntingly, that 'if it contain nothing of amusement . . . it will help to raise the moral tone of our schoolfellows'. It was not for nothing that his peers gave Westcott the nickname 'Miss Waistcoat'. However, the first editorial of the 1856 magazine, of which eight consecutive numbers survive in the school's archives and which are as delightful as they are instructive, is a quite different matter. It asserts in the best eighteenth-century manner that the magazine will 'elevate and refine the tastes of its readers', but more interesting is its aim to seek to be 'a bond of union between the various divisions of our Institution'. Almost twenty years after the move into Barry's building the English School and the Classical School had evidently not yet fully knit together. In order to titillate the

Edwin Hamilton Gifford, Chief Master (1848–62).

appetites of its readers the magazine promises to offer 'Tales and Anecdotes, Reviews, Notices of an interesting and instructive character, Poetry, Verses which have been inserted in "The Book", Charades, Enigmas &c'. It will cost 3*d.* per number or 1*s.*4*d.* per half year. A striking fact about this magazine is the outward-looking nature of most of its material. It is a forum for ambitious writing and not the chronicle that its successor, founded in 1872 and still going strong, was to become. As such it is composed largely of stories, translations (not just, as one would expect, from classical authors but from German as well), poetry, political comment, sketches of important political figures from past and present, excellent correspondence sections dealing with matters of general interest, chess problems and puzzles. Although the verse is, not surprisingly, totally derivative in idiom it is metrically very accomplished and there is one poem, 'Hawleigh Church', which registers a genuinely felt first-hand experience, whilst another is a thoroughly successful exercise in Byron's satirico-comic manner on the subject of *Aeneas in Search of a Home*. All this provides solid evidence that under Gifford there was plenty of intellectual life and bounce in the school.

There is also a lengthy and picturesque account of a cricket match against Bromsgrove School. It is written with great charm and is quite as entertaining as Dickens' famous description of a cricket match in *The Pickwick Papers*. The Bromsgrove captain turns up to toss, smoking a 'real, short, black, cutty pipe', and the King Edward's team lets slip the strong position they were in at lunch by a too careless abandonment to the lavish hospitality that Bromsgrove, with diabolical cunning, provided. The game ends in an honourable draw followed by a brisk session in the bar and a melodious drive back to Birmingham. *Plus ça change* ...! This splendid piece refers to the 1856 fixture but unfortunately the 1857 match is only briefly reported. It was a low-scoring game curtailed by rain which Bromsgrove won by 53 runs – KES 59, Bromsgrove 112.

> The morning opened with a heavy shower of rain, which continued without intermission till about 10.30 a.m. when the wickets were pitched. The batting on the Birmingham side, which had first innings, was very poor, with the exception of Marston, who made the score, and of Kempson; but this may be partly accounted for, by the presence of several new members in our train. The Bromsgrovians showed some very good play, especially Messrs. Cator and Beesly; and the fielding on both sides was excellent, in spite of the unfavourable state of the ground. The game was decided in the first innings, as the rain again commenced, and put a stop to all further proceedings.

This seems a good point at which to introduce the subject of games in the school. Although organised games had played no part in the educational blueprint that Lee had inherited from Arnold it does not mean that cricket, at least, was not played. Jeune had written to the father of one of his boys (the future Sir Francis Galton) to say that his son was playing both cricket and football 'with vigour'. Score books exist of matches played between 1839 and 1842 and a comment on

The Board Room in Barry's building. The large bookcase and its contents were transferred to the Birmingham City Library when the school in New Street was demolished.

one of them records that 'Gibson was sulky and did not try, which perhaps was the reason our fielding was bad'. The diary of a boarder in Lee's house reveals that three of Lee's future Senior Classics played cricket and that they 'did a bit of both', as we now say, and that 'Prince Lee with his wife and daughter, visited the ground while a match was in progress'. But the main problem facing the effective development of games was the fact that the school had no permanent ground. From Lee's time onwards a variety of grounds had been hired for short periods. One ground at Rotton Park had been rented for ten years and the schools had spent some £200 on it but it was then sold to a railway company. This produced a magnificent protest in the fourth number of the new school *Chronicle* in July 1872. Commenting severely on the 'astonishing inactivity' of the cricket club the writer fulminates:

> No match has yet taken place, no practice has been afforded, although most of the clubs in the town have been in active service for some time. The reason is well known. There is no ground for us to play on. Why the railway company should have been allowed to turn a sod of the old ground before a new one had been procured and laid out we cannot tell. It seems as though this was due to the culpable negligence of some party or parties concerned.

We learn from the same article that throughout the 1860s fixtures had been regularly played, against both schools and town clubs with mixed but, on the whole, not very impressive success. (The first recorded match against another school had been against Shrewsbury School in 1854 and had been a creditable draw.) Two issues later the magazine records that 'a field has at length been procured for the education of the School in the sciences of Cricket and Football. The new possession lies on the Bristol Road, at the corner of the Eastern Road ... It is charmingly situated on the banks of the Bourne Brook, a chief tributary of the noble river which beautifies our native town.' This ground at Eastern Road was at first rented and twenty-odd years later bought outright and is still the school's main sports ground, having now been in continuous use by the school for 120 years. And the Bourne Brook still runs alongside it and it remains a very attractive ground indeed. Acquiring this ground solved the problem that Gifford had recognised as pressing eleven years before in 1861. He had then seen how important it was that some kind of provision for physical activity should be made and, because convenient land was difficult to come by, had urged upon the governors a plan to build a gymnasium on the New Street site. He inspected gymnasia in Oxford, at Radley, at Harrow and at the Royal Military College, Woolwich and estimated that what was required would cost £1,500 plus the cost of a part-time instructor. There the matter had rested.

As always there were those who recognised only visible honours as proof that the school was doing well and who were unable to understand that schools are not factories where production quotas can be stabilised, and that in any school glittering university results such as those achieved under Lee can't last for ever. Gifford's pupils certainly did not produce comparable results but they did include Sir Edward Burne-Jones, the artist, and R. W. Dixon who was to teach Gerard Manley Hopkins at Highgate School and was probably the first to recognise his poetic genius. After all, common sense would suggest that the tuition received

The Art Room in Barry's New Street school.

at the university and the actual ability of the boys themselves contributed as much to this situation as the change of Chief Mastership. Complaints on this score were foolish, but more substantial were those directed at the unsatisfactory standard of maths teaching, at the school's poor showing compared with other schools in what were referred to as the 'humbler middle-class examinations' (Oxford Local Examinations) and at the continuing scandal (as it seemed to many) of the governors being an exclusively co-optative body.

The letter which contained these complaints was quoted by Griffith in his *History of the Free Schools etc. of Birmingham* (1861) and it certainly had Gifford in its sights. Its author writes that the school needs a headmaster 'such as Dr. Arnold describes, a man of tact, vigour and force of character, just, impartial, and respecting other interests besides his own'. One cannot really believe that Gifford was deficient in all these qualities, and it sounds very much as if the writer's judgement, for all his information and the probable justice of some of his points, was clouded by an overpowering nostalgia for the glory-days of Lee.

In 1860, towards the end of Gifford's Chief Mastership, the composition of the school was as follows. Apart from the Chief Master and the Second Master there were nine assistant masters, a mathematics master, a composition master, two French masters (both Frenchmen), a German master and four writing-masters. In the Classical School there were twelve classes, the eleventh class being split into two divisions. (Could this have been to avoid an ominous total of thirteen?) Seven masters, including the Chief Master, were responsible for these classes. In the English School there were ten classes in the charge of five masters, two of whom were not in holy orders and one of them not a graduate. There was a total of 457 boys in the school, 246 in the Classical School and 211 in the English School. Five years later there were 462 boys in the school whose parents represented a wide range of occupations as illustrated by the following table:

	Cl. School	Eng. School
Clergy	9	4
Doctors and solicitors	34	5
Manufacturers	10	21
Architects	13	1
Merchants	7	1
Schoolmasters	4	5
Managers and secretaries	14	9
Clerks	9	32
Tradesmen	93	115
Commercial travellers	17	20
Widows	14	25

Interesting facts about these figures are that not far short of half of the total number of boys came from what were designated as 'tradesmen's' families and of that number nearly half again were in the Classical School. The next most numerous group is 'clerks' who beat 'doctors and solicitors' and 'commercial travellers' and 'widows' by a short head.

In January 1862 Gifford became worried about his health and on medical advice went for three months to Torquay. He returned in April but was soon advised by his doctors to retire from the demands of Chief Mastership. The governors generously but perhaps impetuously granted him a pension of £200 a year for life, a decision they came to regret, for retirement from teaching did wonders for his health and he lived to receive his pension for a further forty-three years. In 1884 the governors suggested that perhaps he did not really need the pension, and reminded him that he had offered to relinquish it should he no longer need it, an offer he now had cause to regret. He managed, however, to refuse and relations between the parties became less than cordial. In 1891, by a crowning irony, Oxford University elected him to the seat which they had acquired on the school's governing body. He accepted this offer but was considerate enough not to attend meetings. When he died in 1905 he had been, since resigning from King Edward's, examining chaplain to the bishops of Peterborough and London, Archdeacon of London and Canon of St Paul's and had published a five-volume text and translation of Eusebius. He had also, in 1874, officiated at the marriage of his niece, Emma, to a young man destined to make quite a name for himself. He was called Thomas Hardy.

During the four decades that followed Gifford's strategic withdrawal *pour*

Charles Evans, Chief Master
(1862–72).

mieux sauter elsewhere we can trace three significant developments in the life of the school. They were gradual and spread throughout the Chief Masterships of Gifford's two successors, Charles Evans (1862–72) and Albert Vardy (1872–1900). The first of these was the final resolution, after prolonged and often abrasive conflict, of the problems that had existed for a century or more between the Foundation and the civic authorities. The second was the establishment of science in the school curriculum and the third was the arrival of organised games. It may be tempting at first sight to see the constitutional question as the most important but it would be thoughtless, if only because the school's achievements in science in the present century have been so very impressive. In fact, all three developments were crucial in transforming King Edward's into a modern school that was ready for the new century that was upon it by the end of Vardy's Chief Mastership.

Such institutions as games clubs and the school magazine which, throughout the present century have been stable presences in the life of the school, were, in the middle years of the nineteenth century, much more sporadic. Their existence derived from the energy of particular enthusiasts rather than from an assured place in the pattern of school life. Games, of course, were not compulsory and a subscription of 2s.6d. was required for each club until 1872 when the subscription for the football club was reduced to 1s. In the eight magazines of 1856–7 and the ten magazines of 1872–3 there are frequent pleas for more members of the school to show an interest in both games and magazine.

Reports of games clubs' activities were naturally written by an officer of the club who seeks to ginger up the indifferent majority by a judicious mixture of gloom and hope, a pinch of Jeremiah to season a spoonful of encouraging optimism. In the *K. E. S. Chronicle* of November 1872 the report on the previous cricket season begins thus: 'Now that the cricket season is over, and that of football is commenced, it may be interesting to look back on the doings of our cricketers, and to see whether or not the cricket of the school is going the way of all other institutions'. Although there is ambiguity in this grimly enigmatic announcement it sounds ominous. The writer goes on to mention three matches lost, two won (both against the same school, Tettenhall College) and one drawn. Fowler topped the batting averages with an average of 11.8. (Scores were low in nearly all the school's matches at this time largely, one supposes, because of bad wickets, a common enough hazard in the game at the time.) Discouraging, too, is the stark announcement that 'the second eleven played no matches'. The writer, however, draws consolation for such an indifferent season from the fact that it has afforded 'some hope that if the ground is well attended next year, the school will regain its old position in this manly sport'.

Unfortunately this run of magazines comes to an end before the football season finishes but there is plenty of optimism at the beginning. The school magazine for November 1872 tell us that:

> The opening game of the school was played on the new ground on Saturday afternoon, October 5th, in excellent football weather. The attendance was very numerous indeed, nearly eighty players taking part in the game, a number which strangely contrasts with that of past seasons. We noticed with pleasure, upon the

field, the well-known faces of many old members of the school, who, by their presence, have evidently not forgotten the pleasant games they played during their stay at the school in times gone by.

This seems to have been a practice game in which participants played in relays, for how else can we account for 'eighty players'? It would seem that rugger was not a familiar enough game for everyone to be absolutely sure of the rules – indeed, are they ever? – because the article concludes by observing that 'we think it would not be out of place to give some of the principal laws of the game as played at our school, and we hope all will carefully read them and bear them in mind during play'. Perhaps that 'as played at our school' accounts for the fact that sometimes the team is referred to as 'the sixteen' which would have surprised opponents who had brought only the usual fifteen players. It is clear from subsequent match reports that masters played in the school team, as for example the legendary Rawdon Levett (of whom more later). As reported in the school magazine the exploits of the Revd C. Black against the Queen's College on Saturday, 1 February, were such as to obliterate the efforts of all other members of the side. Three years later, he is still there, playing full-back and taking the place kicks. Many, indeed most, of the football fixtures appear not to have been against other schools but rather against local clubs, some with celebrated names such as Moseley. Others titillate the imagination with their unlikely and thought-provoking names such as Van Wart's Club, with which the school arranged a fixture for 1 March 1873. As the announcement of this fixture appeared in the last magazine of the series the rest is silence.

By the end of the nineteenth century the mathematics at King Edward's School was as distinguished as the classics had been earlier in the century. This development had been gradual. Although several of Lee's brilliant classics had also distinguished themselves in mathematics at Cambridge – three of them, Westcott, Lightfoot and Evans having been Wranglers – it is more than likely that they had received mathematics coaching outside the school. Lee himself could only kindle an interest in mathematics by reading Euclid in Greek but he recognised its importance as a serious school subject, something more than 'casting accounts', and he sought to give it greater prominence in the work of the school. In this endeavour he was much helped by the Second Master, Sydney Gedge, successor to Rann Kennedy, whose twenty-four years at the school (1835–59) did much to establish the subject on a firm base.

Gedge was followed as Second Master by one of Lee's boys, T. N. Hutchinson, who was 'distinguished for scientific and mathematical attainments'. He was of great assistance to both Gifford and Evans in their various grapplings with the difficulties of promoting science and extending mathematics and he left after only five years at the school to found a science department at Rugby School. In the same letter to the governors (30 October 1861) in which he urged the idea of a gymnasium Gifford also pressed for a new chemistry laboratory. He claimed that the size of the existing one was 'quite inadequate to the wants of the class' and, more serious still, 'the most offensive fumes frequently reach the Classical School'. He added that Hutchinson had estimated that 'a suitable laboratory might be erected in a plain style and properly fitted up for about £500'. (For 'in a plain style' read 'cheaply'. Like most Chief Masters seeking to nudge the governors into creative action Gifford was careful to suggest that it wouldn't cost all that much.)

Plans and estimates for building a laboratory and lecture room were prepared by a Mr Hornblower. A passage in his covering letter draws attention to the difficulties that he had encountered in harmonising the new laboratory block with the Gothic style of the main school building; however, he could report that he had solved this problem by concealing the laboratory as much as possible 'by raising the wall of the playground and making it appear to form part of the Railway Station.' Such ingenuity in problem-solving today would win the hearts of CDT teachers everywhere. His plan would cost about £1,000, the governors were unwilling to exceed £800 and so it was ordered that 'further proceedings be suspended for the present'.

At the end of Evans's first term as Chief Master he wrote two important letters to the governors, both dated 1 December 1862. In the first of these he proposed a large and, as he saw it, essential extension in the scope of the school. Prominent in his projected development – which included a lecture room, a library, the creation of a preparatory school and a nightschool – were a chemical laboratory and an engineering-room. Evans, like Gifford, was well aware of the needs of the future. The governors approved his general principles but the Finance Committee advised against the additional expenditure that these plans would entail. However, two years later Evans did manage to secure the appointment of a master specifically to teach 'natural philosophy', i.e. science, in a case where the governors had a mind to appoint an additional mathematics master. At £120 a year the man appointed would be fairly low in the pecking order. A year or two earlier Hunter Smith had been appointed to the Classical School at £180 a year.

Evans's other letter to the governors was about mathematics. He pointed out that although in the Classical School mathematics occupied a quarter of the teaching time it was not a subject of examination for school exhibitions to the universities, which meant that it was not taken as seriously by ambitious boys as it ought to be. He proposed, therefore, that it should count for one-seventh of the marks in the examinations for leavers' exhibitions. He regarded it as '*per se* an essential branch of a liberal education' and observed, interestingly in view of what the future held in store, that 'many boys who have a natural bias to Mathematics (and considerable ability of this kind has always existed in the School) and who might distinguish themselves highly at the Universities, are discouraged ... which ... may prove positively detrimental to the worldly success of our pupils.'

Evans's plan was accepted by the School Committee of the governors (28 April 1863) and it was decreed that the examination should be confined to the 'elementary branches of algebra and geometry' and to include 'plane trigonometry and conic sections'. But then, to ensure that no dilution of the pure classical juice should be countenanced in the matter of leaving exhibitions, a counter-proposal was made that if incitement to mathematical effort were needed a special prize should be offered instead. Evans clearly was not happy with this notion nor were the examiners who, while reporting favourably on the standard of mathematics, also recommended its inclusion in the exhibition examinations. (One would like to think that there had been some very merited collusion with the Chief Master.) The whole business seemed to end in stalemate. But perhaps Evans's greatest service to the cause of mathematics was to come in 1869 when he secured the appointment of Rawdon Levett as mathematics master. In the course of the next thirty-three years Levett was to raise the subject to the very highest level and to exert an enormously vital influence on the whole life of the school. A later Chief Master, Cary Gilson, was to describe him as 'probably the best schoolmaster I have ever known.'

But if, in spite of his notably lucid and convincing arguments, Evans failed to shift the governors in the direction of the eminently sensible changes just mentioned he was more successful in his determination to reform the admission procedure. This was by governors' recommendation and had remained proudly resistant to change or thought since 1552. Evans argued strongly in a letter to the governors (28 April 1863) that admission should be by competitive examination. His arguments, all eminently sensible, made some impact on the governors who went so far as to suggest that it might be possible to combine competitive examination with nomination. By July, however, they had suppressed such recklessness and had come to feel 'after mature deliberation' that competitive examination 'is inexpedient'. As always when this term is used, as it so often is, to put a stop to thought and discussion, there was no hint as to how the conclusion was reached and one is left to make one's own inevitably damaging deductions. But Evans was not a man to give up easily and a good deal of private lobbying may well have gone on because a letter from him to the governors on 20 June 1864 reveals that he had won. The governors had consented to 'place a certain number of vacancies at my disposal for open competition'.

Rawdon Levett (1869–1902), a great mathematics teacher and, from 1890–1902, Second Master.

The first competitive examination was held on 30 August 1864. Candidates still had to be on a governor's list before sitting the examination but it did mean that sub-standard candidates were excluded. There were seventy candidates, ten for the Classical School, of whom two were successful and sixty for the English School, of whom ten were successful. By the time of the next examination, held the following January, the standard of the candidates had risen as twenty-eight out of sixty-two candidates were accepted. In February 1866 the governors agreed that eighty places should be placed at the Chief Master's disposal each year for competitive examination. Evans had got what he wanted and knew to be in the interests of the school. One of his arguments in favour of competitive examinations had been that a collateral advantage would be that they would bring about the creation of more and better preparatory schools and so help towards raising the general standard of education in the town: he was not slow to draw the governors' attention to the fact that this was precisely what happened. His ten years as Chief Master must have contributed greatly to the governors' gradual recognition that taking advice was not necessarily a bad thing. But after ten years he had had enough and at the age of about forty-five he went off to pass his remaining thirty-two years as Rector of Solihull.

Altogether Evans cuts an impressive and agreeable figure. Certainly he was free with the cane but that was par for the course. Like his mentor, Lee, he was an excellent teacher though, one suspects, of a different kind. That difference is suggested by an article in the *Chronicle* just after his departure. The writer notes that the general average of his scholarship success rate was higher than Lee's though there were fewer brilliant successes. 'Of 83 scholarships – the total our school has obtained – 41 have been obtained during a space of 36 years (1830–65) by the pupils of his predecessors, and 42 during a space of eight years (1865–72) by his own'. The quality of mind that had made him a Senior Classic and a Wrangler at Cambridge shows very clearly in his letters to the governors which have an incisiveness and elegant directness of expression that is most refreshing. One of his former pupils, R. H. Giles, wrote a splendid, if slightly nostalgic, account of a sentimental visit to the school which he paid as a middle-aged man. He gives us a vivid picture of Evans in action.

> Old Charlie was always in a hurry. There was so much to be learned; time was so exceedingly precious; heads were so unconscionably thick; caned hands became so scientifically tolerant, that Morning Prayers seemed an insolent intrusion upon the educational liberty of the subject. This used to be the end of our devotional exercise: '. . . be with us all Amen First Class come up'.

Giles describes elsewhere how Evans's eyes 'wore a pained expression of unutterable agony, as though they were regarding the utmost nadir of hopeless ignorance' when a boy forgot a date in a Greek history lesson. His account tells us also of 'the six days' Homeric fight between the champions of the Classic and English Schools'. He hopes that he 'hammered' his adversary well and remembers that he was 'stiff and sore for a week afterwards'. He gives us, too, a vivid picture of Mr Collins, the young master who had won a cricket blue at Cambridge and had been appointed with a view to bracing up the school's performance at 'this manly sport'.

> I came to the class-room where, under Mr. Tom Collins, I began life as a fresh herring. One of our tribe had a curious habit of drawing his hand over the wall as he endeavoured to elucidate the mysteries of 'Delectus', and the room seemed to echo Mr. Collins invariable protest, 'Fostah, Sah, don't paw the wall, Sah'.

(As a matter of passing interest, the term 'fresh herring' to describe a first-year boy became corrupted to 'sherring' and in that form is still current in the school.) Giles also tells us that contributors paid for the printing costs of their contributions to the *Chronicle* – 'a most salutary rule' as he says – and that the magazine was born in the Library which was, in reality, a private study room for the exclusive use of the First Class. There, they 'held debate upon high imperial policy' and 'settled the Eastern Question, demolished the Irish Church Bill, and kicked the Turk out of the map at a single sitting'. He writes, too, with affection of the French master, M Vincent, of Mr Klugh and of the Revd 'Jimmy' Yates but with rather less warmth of J. Hunter Smith. According to Rawdon Levett, when he came to the school in 1869 the crowded classrooms resounded with 'war cries, and cries, too, of the wounded that recalled the Battle of Prague' and an Old Edwardian, Joseph Manton, refers to the school under Evans as 'largely governed by old-fashioned and severe methods'. Nevertheless it does not seem to have been at all a bad place; there was certainly plenty of life about it.

7

The Golden Age?

Here no classic grove secludes us, here abides no cloister'd calm,
Not the titled nor the stranger wrestles here to gain the palm;
Round our smoke-encrusted precinct labour's turbid river runs,
Builders of this burly city temper here their strenuous sons.

King Edward's School Song

'STRENUOUS' IS NOT, perhaps, the adjective that springs unbidden to the lips of
those of us who have laboured, last period on a Thursday afternoon, to inculcate
habits of good learning in the sons of the burly city's builders. Yet the stanza
quoted above encapsulates exquisitely the way in which Birmingham liked,
indeed still likes, to see itself. The desire to keep fops at a distance goes back,
as we have seen, to the earliest years of the school's history and idlers had not
had an easy time since Jeune's volcanic advent. However, in spite of the myth-
making potency of school songs when one comes to examine the life of the school
in what is sometimes thought of as its golden age it bears a distressing
resemblance to that of other comparable schools. The facts of life for the
supposedly rugged, industrious sons of the burly city are much as they are for
any schoolboy — whether he can cope with his work, how is he to get off the
hook for being late with his prep for the third time this term, will he be picked
for the school team, how incomprehensible/interesting/boring/entertaining/
chaotic/demanding Mr You-Know-Who's periods are, and what a twit/
bastard/laugh/dynamo/nice-guy/slave-driver old So-and-So is. From such a
point of view the years during which Evans's two successors, Albert Vardy
(1872–1900) and Robert Cary Gilson (1900–29), presided over the school
seemed years of security, stability and success but as we shall see later it was not
quite as simple as that.

It had been in Evans's time, in 1864 to be precise, that a train of events began
that was to culminate nearly twenty years later in a major reorganisation of the
Foundation. In that year the government set up the Schools Enquiry Commission
— an event which wonderfully concentrated the mind of many a governing body

and, indeed, of many a headmaster. At the same time a group of prominent Birmingham citizens founded the Free Grammar School Association with the aim of securing reforms in the Foundation. Their attitude towards the governors was much more moderate and realistic than that of the Birmingham Town Council which simply wanted to take over the governing body. The Commission, in the person of T. H. Green, a distinguished Oxford philosopher, came to Birmingham in 1866 and heard evidence from the governors, from Evans, from the Town Council and from the Free Grammar School Association. Many of the Commission's recommendations were acceptable to the governors and, in fact, reinforced the suggestions that Evans had been making, but others found the governors adamantinely opposed – that boarding should be abolished, that non-clerical masters should be employed and, above all, that they themselves should cease to be an entirely self-electing body.

It would be tedious to follow all the manœuvres between the interested parties that occupied the intervening years until 1883 when an accommodation was finally achieved, but one incident may well be mentioned. In 1872 an Endowed Schools Commission proposed a scheme which was not only unacceptable to the governors but also ran counter to the suggestions of the School Enquiry Commission. The new Chief Master, Albert Vardy, swung into action with a powerful letter to Lord Lyttelton, Chief Endowed Schools Commissioner; then he deployed in support the literary power of a terrifying body of intellectual commandos drawn from the ranks of old boys and former masters – Evans, Gifford, Linwood, Westcott, Lightfoot, Benson, Hutchinson and others. His lordship must have been relieved that Jeune and Prince Lee had both died a year or two earlier. The scheme was demolished but the manner of its demolition outraged the party for reform outside the school, and Vardy and the governors came to see that a mutually acceptable solution to these differences had to be found. To this end Vardy worked tirelessly and the reorganisation of 1883 owed a great deal to his patience and persuasiveness.

The final outcome, arrived at by stages, was as follows: boarders abolished; non-clerical masters allowed; competitive examinations and fee-paying established; the headmaster to be called Headmaster; a High School for Girls to be established; the Classical and English Schools to become a High School for Boys; the Middle School for boys (developed from the former Elementary Schools) to be upgraded to become a chain of grammar schools throughout the city; the composition of the governing body to be reformed so that there should be a total of 21 governors, 8 nominated by the Town Council, 9 co-opted and 4 nominated as follows, one by each of Cambridge, Oxford and London Universities and one by the Foundation teachers. This solution to the anomalies and antagonisms that had hitherto bedevilled the Foundation owed most to four men, to Evans and Vardy within the school and to T. H. Green and C. E. Matthews outside the school. The two latter men both became valuable governors, having been, in Green's case the government-appointed commissioner to investigate the school in 1866, and in Matthews's case one of the school's most eloquent and rational critics. But for all that the solution was reasonable and forward-looking and showed the governing body prepared to shoulder their

The head boy of KES and the head girl of KEHS present an address and flowers to Queen Victoria on the occasion of a Royal visit to Birmingham, in celebration of her jubilee.

responsibilities towards the city as well as towards the Free Grammar School it was in time to prove beyond the Foundation's resources. A governors' Minute of February 1866 had noted that 'whatever desirable schemes may be suggested in reference to other classes of children ... they would be too dearly purchased at the cost of lowering the standard of the present Classical or English School or in any way impairing their efficiency'. The financial prognosis of 1883 turned out to be sadly optimistic and created a dilemma which the governors of the 1920s were to seek desperately to resolve – how to find the money to fund two High Schools and five grammar schools.

This danger was not, however, apparent to those involved in the buoyant life of the school during Vardy's Chief Mastership. The feeling of well-being and stability that one senses in the school at that time was not just a reflection of a national mood but was the result of the personalities of its leading figures, not only of Vardy himself but of masters who, to paraphrase Hutton's words, sank their personalities in the school they had adopted.

From 1869 until 1902, that is to say throughout Vardy's entire Chief Mastership, Rawdon Levett taught mathematics at King Edward's School. The fact that he was a fine teacher who combined intellectual edge with inspirational enthusiasm meant that his pupils achieved the kind of success at Cambridge that Lee's pupils had achieved in classics almost fifty years earlier. Twenty of his pupils became Wranglers and, as Hutton points out, 'at one time the Senior Mathematical Masters at Eton, Harrow and Winchester were all Old Edwardians, Levett's pupils'. Success brings prestige and from Levett's time onwards mathematics rated with classics as a high-prestige subject. He was, however, rather more than a fine teacher; he was involved in a multitude of school activities, rugger in his early days, societies, the founding of the School Club, contributing to the cost of the pavilion on the Eastern Road ground and working to create the Old Edwardian's Association. For twelve years he was Second Master.

One who laboured even longer (1861–1901) in the Edwardian vineyard was

Rawden Levett with his A1 maths set of 1894. All except two won an open scholarship to Oxford or Cambridge.

The witty, caustic, stimulating John Hunter Smith, Assistant Master (1861–1901).

John Hunter Smith who taught the Fourth Class. Like Levett he was remarkable as a teacher and as a personality. Witty, explosive, inspirational, he was, we are told, 'to the respectable middle-class Philistine incomprehensible and, at times, detestable, for he was chiefly occupied in demolishing the fetishes of that worthy person'. He was also president of the Old Edwardian's Literary Section, an activity which has subsequently been choked to death in the jungle of those very fetishes. A year before Hunter Smith's retirement and two years before Levett's C. H. Heath arrived to teach classics. His arrival in 1900 coincided with that of a new Chief Master, Cary Gilson, and he stayed two years longer, retiring in 1931. Apart from his teaching he was a great games enthusiast and was one of the original housemasters when houses were first created in the school (artificially, of course) as a basis for games. It is not surprising and it is only just that when, in the early 1950s, houses ceased to be called by the current housemaster's name and were given permanent names, the names of Heath and Levett should have been chosen along with those of six former Chief Masters. It might be mentioned in passing that if service to the school be the criterion of selection it is both odd and sad that Brokesby was omitted; it could well be argued that he has a much greater claim to inclusion in this roll-call of worthies than Gifford.

Vardy himself was something of a new model among Chief Masters. Like his predecessors he had, of course, a first in classics at Cambridge and although he lacked the academic panache of Lee and Evans he retained, we are told, 'a real though sober respect' for academic distinction and was 'a very sound scholar of the old type'. But it was other qualities that gave a distinctly new look to his Chief Mastership, his negotiating skills, the range of activities over which they were employed, both in the city and nationally, and above all the personal impact which he made on all who met him. Joseph Manton, a boy under Vardy and

82

later a master at the school, describes him in a way that contrasts strongly with his predecessor. 'He was a short, thick-set man' (unlike Evans who was tall and graceful, but like Lee) 'generally wearing heavy boots and planting his feet very firmly. He wore an ordinary turn-down collar and a white bow-tie and never a clerical hat. When I first knew him he had black side-whiskers ... He seldom raised his voice; his rebukes were solemn, never hasty or exaggerated; he was always punctual, never in a hurry, always deliberate, never flurried ... He had a pleasant smile but his eyes never sparkled with delight ... [he] had found a school largely governed by old-fashioned and severe methods; he transformed it into one in which his mere presence secured order and obedience.' A great dictum of his was that 'schools exist mainly for the average boy'. Hunter Smith wrote of him that 'he left a Day School endowed with nearly all the virtues, and none of the vices, of one of the great Boarding Schools of the country'.

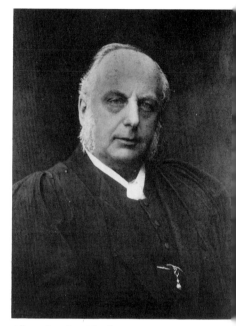

Albert Vardy, Chief Master (1872–1900).

Vardy was described as 'a heaven-born chairman' in which role his incisive intellect was supplemented by the diplomatic virtues of patience, tact and common sense. A greater contrast with Lee could scarcely be imagined. In his first year (1872) Vardy invited the newly formed Headmasters' Conference (1869) to hold its annual meeting at King Edward's School, thereby cementing the school's membership which had begun the previous year. He was largely responsible for the foundation in Birmingham in 1874 of the Teachers' Association and he came to be seen as 'an unofficial Bishop of Education in one of the largest cities of the Empire'. Above all he was 'revered' by his fellow teachers – not always the good fortune of headmasters – and no wonder, for he took the lower classes of the school as well as the Classical Sixth and was a great help to assistant masters and not only pedagogically. His successful mobilisation of powerful opposition to the proposals of the Schools Enquiry Commission of 1872 led to the defeat of the Bill which embodied them and, as a result of this defeat, assistant masters did not get the salary increase that they had been expecting. With a splendid mixture of delicate understanding and shrewd political sense Vardy resigned £400 a year of his own salary to augment theirs, on the condition that the governors matched it. Determination and clear-sighted attachment to what he saw as the proper educational course and a skilful tact in handling both governors and teachers are seen to combine in this episode which distils the essential strength of his whole Chief Mastership. But he suffered the cancer of success, to be in permanent demand on all manner of committees, with the result that, as he never skimped anything, he worked himself to death. The *Journal of Education* wrote of him:

> On the day on which he was first seized with illness he had been entertaining a party of local headmasters to luncheon, he had addressed the parents of the new boys, he had been discussing the operations of the new Church College, and had an interview with the Committee of Middlemore's Homes for Boys, in which he always took an active interest. Meantime, school exercises were awaiting his perusal, and papers from the candidates for Holy Orders, for he was Examining Chaplain to the Bishop of Worcester.

His memorial brass in the beautiful village church of Lapworth, midway between Birmingham and Warwick, describes him with felicitous accuracy as 'a wise educator, devoted teacher, lavish of service ... revered, beloved'. Photographs of him show the black side-whiskers turned to white. He was only fifty-eight when he died in harness, having spent almost half his life as Chief Master of King Edward's School. In him the guru became a fully human being.

A contemporary wrote that the school under Vardy was characterised by 'a cheerful seriousness' and that 'it was unsectarian, little frequented by the uncultured wealthy'. In it plenty of work was done and few 'bloods', i.e. 'uncultured wealthy', were to be found, Birmingham being an uncongenial habitat for the growth of the species. In an age before the mania for school uniforms ensured that personal choice in dress can only be exercised in the matter of underwear, members of KES wore what they liked to school. Straw hats, bowlers and various types of cap diversified the scene and, in the 1890s, soft hats along with brown boots appeared, both seen, one suspects, as the mark of the potential cad. An enterprising tradesman sold a small silver badge which some boys wore on bowler or boater to signal their membership of the school. There was a school tie but, according to Manton, 'it was seldom seen'. A letter to the school magazine described one boy's tie as 'a Bulgarian atrocity'. 'We looked', wrote Manton, 'a nondescript lot'. But they were a nondescript lot who were 'distinguished by a spirit of earnest studiousness and originality of thought'. They delighted in watching very recent old boys 'who had been no great shakes at school, promenading on the other side of New Street on Saturday mornings' advertising their liberated manhood in a frock-coat and top-hat. The absence of uniforms was paralleled by an absence of prefects (an innovation that Lee had not thought necessary to import from Rugby), though we learn that 'the School Captain was an important person'.

As a young member of the first eleven Manton was 'often astonished or even alarmed at the liberties they [senior boys] took on railway journeys in disregarding regulations and officials ... No master journeyed with us on our out-matches; we were quite independent of any out-of-school supervision and masters did not very often visit the school field.' It is clear that games counted

The school rugger XV, 1892–3.

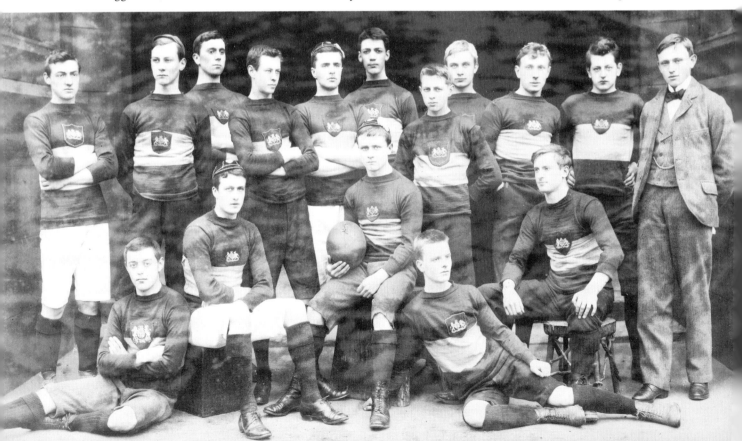

This looks very much like a victorious house cricket squad, comprising both junior and senior teams. The housemaster is obviously Measures and the period pre-1914.

for little in the educational programme of the school, and this is perhaps the more surprising as it was precisely in these decades that the dynamic of 'manliness' had supplanted that of 'godliness' in the life of so many schools. Yet although Vardy had literally no time for games he gave the first eleven time off to go to see W. G. Grace when the great man was playing in Birmingham. Games, of course, were not compulsory and were not to become so until after the Second World War but Sir Richard Hopkins recalls that gymnastics were. In the 1890s, he tells us, the gym was large and well-equipped and was much used. The instructor, Mr Hubbard, 'already advanced in years', nevertheless amazed the audience at a gym display 'by a double somersault from a flying trapeze'. Even more astonishing is the fact that twenty years later Hubbard was still in charge of gymnastics though, mercifully, from the safety of a chair.

Revd E. W. Badger, assistant master (1880–1912).

As we move into the era of Vardy's successor, Robert Cary Gilson (1900–29), we encounter a man who was not only remarkable but is still with us in the memories of many a living Old Edwardian. One of them, Norman Craig, who left school in 1930, returned later in the decade as a master and remained until his retirement in 1976, wrote of Gilson in the *OE Gazette*, 'In my years at Cambridge . . . all men seemed puny compared with him. In everything he was original without being a crank. He was a great man, but not because he was headmaster of King Edward's. He was a great man who happened to be headmaster of King Edward's'.

Craig's conviction of Gilson's eminence is echoed by almost everyone who knew him or has written about him. When at Cambridge himself Gilson had slipped a first in natural sciences between firsts in both parts of the classical tripos. He also read for the Bar. In his house he fitted up a laboratory and a workshop in which he delighted to create labour-saving gadgets for domestic use. He was an experienced and skilful climber in the early days of that pastime and on his death the Alpine Society published a slim memorial pamphlet. He was fluent in

Gilson and his Common Room in 1906. Acatos is second from the left in the middle row, Heath and Measures at the opposite end of the same row. Davidson is second from the left in the front row and Badger next to Gilson to the right. Unlike most modern group photographs it is full of human beings.

Below: Robert Cary Gilson, Chief Master (1900–29). A marvellously true and expressive photograph.

several modern languages and was no mean mathematician. No wonder Craig said recently (1991) 'I still dream of Gilson.' He tells us that Gilson 'had a magnificent head' and 'that there was a twinkle in his eye which could be detected if one dared to penetrate behind his majestic mien and booming voice'. He obviously possessed the same sort of calm, magisterial authority as Vardy. Both the authority and the humour were shown in the incident when a boy who stood 6ft.7½in. in his socks complained that he felt embarrassed (understandably) at having to wear a school cap. Gilson issued a decree that all boys over 6ft.6in. in height were excused from wearing the school cap. His successor, England, would have made a tremendous issue of principle out of the request whereas Gilson hit upon a witty way to circumvent the collision between common sense and obedience to school rules.

Many of the masters during Gilson's time are as alive in living minds as he is himself. They have been described as 'remarkable for their sturdy idiosyncrasies'. Harmlessly eccentric in Gilson's first decade was Brewerton, a veteran classics master. A nonagenarian OE writes that 'under Brewy we stood round in an open square and were moved up and down according to our deserts. There was always a chance of being told to "go to the bottom for a fool".' There was a legend of a boy who replied politely 'I'll do anything for a fool, sir', and was promptly told to 'go top'. At the same time T. J. Baker was giving science the prestige of maths and classics and establishing a department that has subsequently achieved superlative excellence. He was followed by Cmdr. Langley who taught chemistry and was a school institution. A letter written to him by the mother of Dennis Knight, shot down and lost in the sea off Malta in 1941, is touching testimony to the degree to which he was liked and admired. He became Second Master and Acting Headmaster in the interregnum during the

Second World War. Charles Davidson and 'Black Dick' Richards maintained the momentum of mathematical excellence that Levett had set going and another fine mathematician, though much less successful as a teacher was H. R. Smith, known as 'Tatcho'. This unlikely sobriquet was the brand name of some kind of hair oil or hair restorer and was applied with devastatingly simple schoolboy irony to Smith in view of the fact that he was bald. A particularly brilliant member of Gilson's common room was M. J. Acatos who taught modern languages. One of his pupils and subsequently his successor as head of the subject, Jim Biggs, used to claim that at times he taught three groups simultaneously, each group learning a different language. One cannot say whether the bravura of this feat was a consequence of time-tabling or simply the delight of a virtuoso revelling in his own powers. He was a friend of the concert pianist, Benno Moiseiwich and a fine amateur pianist himself. The Revd W. Sneath (the Bishop), Captain Kirby ('the Pink 'Un'), 'Bruiser' Baines, Bryant ('the Bargee') and, of course, C. H. Heath, were all vivid presences in Gilson's school and exist as powerful mythological figures in the memory of many an elderly OE.

Yet the apparent stability of the school at this time was somewhat illusory. The authority of Gilson's personality concealed the fact that all was not entirely well with the Foundation. Its ills, like 'th'imposthume of much wealth and peace' noted by Hamlet, were also in danger of breaking inward. The financial crisis hinted at on a previous page was upon the Foundation. The expense of funding two High Schools and five grammar schools had proved too great. The grammar schools had entailed a capital expenditure of £170,000 and, in spite of its considerable income, by 1919 the Foundation had run up a deficit of £40,000. Moreover, the financial projections for the next few years were not encouraging. The Finance Committee of the governing body proposed two possible courses of action to reduce this deficit. The first was to disencumber the Foundation of two of the grammar schools; these, it was proposed, should be taken over by the local authority which already supported nine or ten grammar schools in the city. The second was to apply to the local authority for a grant which would then be supplemented by a grant from central government. The full governing body objected to the second proposal on the grounds that it would reduce their freedom of action in the future and 'hamper them in fulfilling the responsibilities which they have discharged for so many generations, and which are defined in their Act of Parliament'. They foresaw that a consequence of accepting help from the local authority would be to accord that authority a share in the government of the Foundation. So they decided to adopt the first option and jettison two of their grammar schools. This was in line with the thinking of their Minute of 1866 quoted on p.81.

The decision, however, soon brought trouble. In the first place the plan was something of a halfway house; the saving made by unloading only two grammar schools was not enough. In the second place the local authority found the idea, as it stood, unacceptable, and in the third place an important body of public opinion was soon found to be hostile. In their thirty-odd years of existence the Foundation grammar schools had generated a great deal of loyalty and *esprit de corps*. A deputation of their former pupils presented to the governors a petition

Charles Davison, senior mathematics master, flanked by his two star pupils, both Senior Wranglers, A. W. Ibbotson and P. J. Daniell. Ibbotson was subsequently knighted after a career in the Indian Civil Service and Daniell became Professor of Mathematics at Sheffield.

C. H. Heath (1900–31), teacher of classics and housemaster. Compiler of the Record of Edwardians who served in the First World War.

Hunter Smith's classroom in the
New Street building, June 1895.

with some 6,000 signatures against the proposed transfer and parents and former
pupils of Handsworth Grammar School registered their solid opposition at a
public meeting. In the face of these two unmistakable expressions of public
feeling the governors changed course. They decided to adopt the alternative
scheme, to apply to the local authority for a grant-in-aid and to bite on the bullet
of whatever conditions it entailed.

The conditions proposed to secure the Foundation a grant of £35,000 were
certainly a considerable constraint on the governors' freedom of action. Their
audited accounts had to be submitted to the local authority as did their estimates;
their salary scales and the salaries paid had to be submitted also and they could
not alter salaries without approval; they had to co-operate with the local
authority over pupil's age of admission and the conditions for free places; they
had to allow access to any officer of the local authority at all reasonable times;
they had to admit representatives of the local authority to the governing body;
the local authority admitted no responsibility for deficits. It is clear that these
terms constituted a severe limitation of the governors' autonomy, and it was
ironic that, having been freed from the constriction of the Charity
Commissioners by an Act of Parliament in 1900, the Foundation should now be
submitting to that which resulted from accepting a grant from the City Council.

In the event the scheme did not prove a complete success. But it was not so
much the limitation of independence in return for a grant of £35,000 that led
to renewed negotiation as the fact that escalating costs rendered the amount of
the grant inadequate to the needs of seven schools. So a further scheme was
devised which was known as the 'deficiency grant'. Each year the amount of
calculated income from fees and endowments would be subtracted from the
estimates of expenditure and the balance would be found by the City Council.
Estimates had to be accepted by that body and any over-expenditure had first to

be approved by them. Driven by necessity to the position of a dependent relative the governors had inevitably to put up with some loss of autonomy which, as the years passed, they found increasingly irksome as it inhibited development precisely as the old constraints of the Charity Commission had done. It was this not very happy solution to the Foundation's financial difficulties that, during the final decade of Gilson's imperial sway, concealed the permanent threat to its long-term health.

At this time the Upper School consisted of three upper and three lower sixth forms and three upper and three lower fifth forms; the Middle School of three upper and two lower middles; and the Lower School of two removes and two shells, two fourths and two thirds. General opinion seems to be that teaching in the lower school was not good as too many masters seemed to suppose that explanation was an unnecessary luxury. Exception from this criticism must be made in favour of 'Codger' Power who was able to relate to the wavelength of boys in the first year. Teaching the 'playmates' in his room called the Power House he would play gramophone records to entertain his boys as they worked, taking care to use a fibre needle whose soft tone would ensure that the sound did not reach the ears of the Chief Master. One OE writes of these years that he can remember 'no irksome rules and regulations'. School uniform did not exist. Only the school cap was compulsory and some sixth-formers used (successfully) to ignore this requirement and come to school in a soft hat. Life was easy-going and Gilson himself once spoke of 'the reasonableness of King Edward's'. But it was because of his own immense personal authority that he was able to run so successful a school on so light a rein.

It was in Gilson's time that both the school's Cadet Corps and its Dramatic Society were instituted. There had been both 'drilling' and plays in the nineteenth century but neither activity was a permanent feature of school life. In 1865 a corps had been formed to be attached to the 1st Warwickshire Rifle

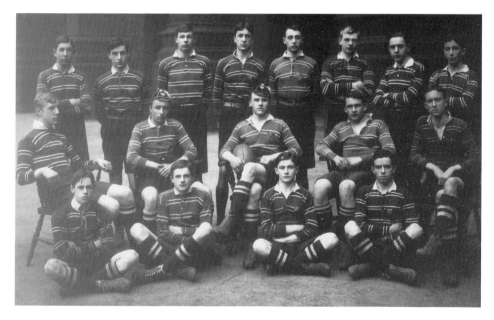

The school's 1st XV for the 1910–11 season. J.R.R. Tolkien is on the extreme right of the centre row. (Picture by courtesy of Fr. John Tolkien).

A group in the production of Henry IV Part I of 1924. Styles have changed somewhat since.

The KES cadet corps going to camp from Snow Hill Station, *c.* 1925.

Volunteers and Tom Collins made its commanding officer with the rank of captain. But it did not last and the Cadet Corps was not put on a regular footing until 1907. The institution of a regular dramatic society had to wait until after the Great War, until 1921 in fact. Its purpose was the annual performance of a school play which soon settled into the annual performance of a play by Shakespeare, about which more will be said later. As for the cadet corps, Gilbert Price, a boy at school between 1912 and 1915 and still going strong, writes of field-days with other schools, 'I never had a clear idea of what was happening, but so long as I had plenty of blank ammunition I was happy'. He mentions, too, that at the annual camp on Salisbury Plain in August 1914 'Talbot, the chaplain, preached a sermon in which he compared Europe to the man in the parable who built greater barns and prepared to eat, drink and be merry, only to be told that that night his soul would be required of him'. As we look back on this notably happy period in the school's history it is easy to forget that it encloses the carnage of the Great War, a war in which 1,412 OEs served and 254 lost their lives, 9 won the MC and Bar, 101 the MC and 10 the MM, and two masters lost their sons, Tatcho Smith and Gilson himself.

One of the obituary notices for Vardy in the *OE Gazette* had spoken of 'the awe that surrounds the head of a great school'. The phrase exemplifies beautifully the tendency to see headmasters as gurus that seems to have been peculiarly

characteristic of the phase of English education initiated by Arnold in 1828. On the whole our own century – and particularly its second half – has neither produced nor wanted such figures; the desiderata for its models of academic authority are managerial skills and 'efficiency' rather than learning and 'wisdom'. But if, at King Edward's, the authentic *je ne sais quoi* of the real guru had not quite been felt in the personalities of Gifford and Evans it certainly had in those of Lee, Vardy and Gilson. The latter was unmistakably in the tradition. As he walked from the station to the school in his grey overcoat and woollen gloves, or to lunch at his reserved table in the restaurant of Marshall & Snelgrove Gilson would be pointed out in awed tones to visitors to the city. Self-conscious Birmingham could recognise one of its most distinguished ornaments.

A group of OE officers during the 1914–18 war. Clive Assinder is on the left of the back row.

91

8

Upheaval

The old order changeth, yielding place to new

Tennyson: *Morte D'Arthur*

To MANY GILSON's retirement in 1929 seemed like 'a breach in nature/For ruin's wasteful entrance'. His successor, Edwin England, had, like four of his five immediate predecessors, read classics at Trinity College, Cambridge. Like Gifford, eighty years earlier, he had to follow a great predecessor but unlike Gifford he was not a young man of twenty-eight. He was forty-nine when he took up this, his fourth headmastership, the first Chief Master since Price in 1776 for whom the Chief Mastership of King Edward's School was not his first headship.

He came to a school that had a very strong sense of its own identity and achievements and was with good reason very sure of itself. But with the benefit of hindsight we can see, perhaps, that the situation was not quite as straightforward as may at first appear. Some of its slightly less than rosy features would probably have been apparent to England fairly soon after he arrived: the sheer difficulty of having to follow so admired and venerated a predecessor; the financial constraints that compelled dependence on the City Council and thus restricted freedom of action; the increasingly apparent inadequacy of the school buildings. But one may suspect that there was another factor present that was by no means as easy to identify. There is a point in the life of all eminent and successful institutions where achievement may begin to be undermined by the insidious onset of self-congratulation. What appeared to contemporaries as the preordained certainty with which school life moved along its appointed grooves during Gilson's last decade may appear to posterity more like flying on automatic pilot. It was not so much a matter of individuals thanking God that they are not as other men are as of an institution's collective certainty that its ways are the best ways and 'there's an end on't'. It may well be a decade or more before such a debilitating complacency begins to show as a lower level of vitality in the institution as a whole, yet one cannot help feeling that King Edward's School may have been near this perilous point at about the time of England's arrival. However, the upheavals and crises of the next two decades, in claiming immediate attention, delayed recognition of this underlying malaise and it is to them that we must soon attend. But first, a look at life in the school in its last years in New Street.

The fact that New Street Station was adjacent to the school made it difficult to secure the 'cloister'd calm' which the author of the school song, Alfred Hayes, seemed to regard as unnecessary for strenuous Edwardians and liable to produce spineless shin-rubbers. Its proximity constituted a permanent temptation to exhibitionists to demonstrate their daring by climbing on its roofs. In other ways, too, the railway was an inescapable feature of the daily routine. Because a large number of boys came to school by train the times of starting and finishing the day were geared to railway timetables, and there was a long midday break between 12.30 and 2.45 to allow boys to travel home to lunch. Ford, the head porter, knew which train every boy in the school travelled by and in this, no doubt, facilitated the identification of those whose behaviour on the trains had ruffled members of the public. Rowland Ryder recalls that even Enoch Powell was, if not involved in, at least touched by such goings-on. 'I must,' wrote Ryder in a newspaper article in 1971, 'have travelled to or from New Street in the same compartment as Powell well over a hundred times. Never once in those four years did I hear him speak ... I was once indulging some mild horse-play when I was flung against him as he was reading in a corner seat. I was terrified and apologised profusely. He grunted amiably and went on with his reading.'

E.T. England, Chief Master (1929–41), giving out a notice from Sapientia.

A no less exciting temptation than climbing on the roof of the station was offered by the even closer proximity of King Edward's High School for Girls. Since 1896, thirteen years after its inception, it had occupied a site adjoining the New Street school, on land formerly occupied by a hotel prophetically named the Hen and Chickens. Not only 'particular friendships' – as they are called in monastic communities – but contact of any kind between boys and girls was discouraged and carried with it the risk of grave rebuke and severe correction. One unfortunate girl was hauled over the coals for coming to school escorted by one of the boys. The fact that he turned out to be her brother only slightly mitigated their joint indiscretion, hers in being in male company and his in being male. In a phrase to treasure England warned the boys against 'miscellaneous sparking'.

Not all boys went home to lunch and for those who did not the centre of the city provided a variety of delights with which to while away two hours and a quarter. One such was the weekly organ recital in the Town Hall by the City organist, G. D. Cunningham. A different entertainment was provided by the tub-thumpers in the Bull Ring, Birmingham's equivalent to Speaker's Corner in Hyde Park. Ryder remembers in particular one regular operator, an ex-policeman from Hereford, who sought to convince passers-by that he was the true heir to the throne. He based this interesting assertion on the shrewdly thought-out claim that he was descended from one of Henry VIII's bastards and had, he said, written to King George V to keep him informed of developments. He had not yet received an answer.

Had not so many boys gone home to lunch this long lunch-break would have been an ideal time for meetings of the school societies that proliferated during this decade. In 1929 the only activities that were dignified with an entry in the Blue Book were the Literary Society and the Debating Society. In that publication secretaries of these two organisations, along with the Librarian and Editor of the *Chronicle*, were to be found in the elevated company of secretaries and captains of games. Ten years later the Blue Book for September 1939 records in addition the names of the secretaries of the Musical, Dramatic, Arts and Crafts, Scientific, Photographic, Archaeological, Geographical, Philatelic and Junior Debating Societies, nine new societies in ten years. This does not mean, of course, that no interest had been shown in these pursuits before, but rather that such interest had now grown to a point where it needed canalising. The existence of what may be called an 'official' society meant that a boy with that particular interest knew from the start where and how he could pursue it in the context of school life.

Within the school non-academic hierarchies existed. One of these made itself felt in the conventions governing the use of initials – most important in an age when first names were hardly ever used, except possibly by very close friends. A boy's initials were placed before his surname only if he were a member of the first eleven or first fifteen; otherwise initials followed the surname. This conferred gentlemanly status on such eminent characters by imitating the current fashion in printing cricket scores, whereby gents were distinguished from players by just such a method. At Monday morning school-prayers after a weekend match, these same august personages lined up and strode masterfully out of Big School before the admiring eyes of all the lesser mortals. Moreover, in contrast to the situation in Vardy's time, prefects had now been for many years a prominent feature of school life and there was, perhaps, an ominous symbolism in the fact that when the whole school was gathered together the prefects stood facing the assembled multitude, a decidedly confrontational arrangement. At a later date, after the move to Edgbaston, their positioning at morning prayers was to make them look even more like prison warders, as they then formed a long row across the front of Big School confronting the whole school, masters included. Were they, one may have wondered, the thin blue line keeping back the lesser breeds without the law or a riot squad ready to move in? Either way, it was an arrangement that ensured that timid sherrings and bolshie fifth-formers knew the facts of life, and it was not changed until the 1970s.

During the 1930s the strong common-room personalities who had given the school so much of its individuality during the two previous decades passed into retirement. A school is to some extent defined by the personalities of its teachers and Acatos, Heath, Kirby, Richards, Sneath, Marples, Maclardy, 'Tatcho' Smith and the Second Master, Tom Baker, who all retired between 1931 and 1936, had acted as defining agents in this way. But at the same time a new group was

E.V. Smith, Chief Mathematics Master (1933–70), Second Master (1945–70).

forming that was to be the nucleus of a rather different common room in the two decades after the Second World War. Roger Dunt, Tom Burgess, Eric Williams and Frank Kay constituted the basis of a classics department that needed to fear comparison with none, likewise E. V. Smith, Jack Roberts, Maurice Porter and Norman Craig in mathematics and Jim Biggs, Bill Barlow and Ted Leeds in modern languages. Two scientists, Bill Hall and Bernard Guy, were appointed, each of whom subsequently became emperor of an ever-expanding and phenomenally successful department, and at the very end of England's Chief Mastership Charles Blount came to be head of history. They were all young men when appointed and most of them came to stay. With the exception of Tom Burgess, who became headmaster of one of the Foundation grammar schools in 1951 and Bill Hall who went to Kenya in 1952, they were to be dominant personalities during the 1950s and 1960s.

Several OEs report that the ethos of the school at this time was very examination-centred. In spite of the vigorous life of school societies (particularly the Debating Society), in spite of the activities of the Cadet Corps and the

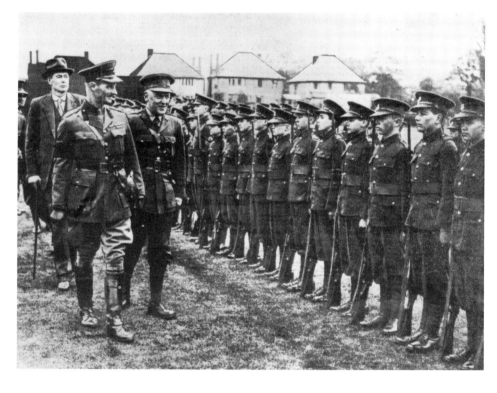

CCF inspection on the Eastern Road playing field some time between January 1936 and September 1939. The inspecting officer is Colonel E.G. Gidley-Kitchin and the Chief Master in pursuit is E.T. England.

formation of a school scout troop, in spite of flourishing cricket and rugger teams, as far as work was concerned non-examination subjects were not taken seriously, in the sixth forms particularly. Intellectually, reports a former Bishop of Bermuda, Fr Anselm Genders, who was in the Classical Sixth during the last years in New Street, the school was narrow-minded, a view which is borne out by the experience of others.

One suspects that England did not feel easy in the relaxed atmosphere bequeathed to him by Gilson. The latter had been largely invisible except for each morning's appearance in Big School. The school had answered to a series of Olympian directives that emanated from the cigar smoke of his library. England, on the other hand, preferred to walk about (like the appropriately named and legendary Walker of St Paul's) and was liable to drop in on any master's lesson without asking leave. Such a habit, combined with a personality often described as 'remote and austere', did not make him easy to live with. One OE feels that England was 'always against something' – the creation of a Rationalist Society, for example, or a particular editorial in the *Chronicle*. To many people he appeared to make mountains out of molehills and to lack a sense of humour. It was not that he was incapable of dry remarks. (For instance, during the school's evacuation to Repton, he warned the boys against going into a derelict farm building on an adjacent property as the roof was unsafe, adding, 'If you enter the barn on your head be it – as it probably will.' In the confusion of the first weeks at Repton when nobody quite knew where he was supposed to be England advised the Common Room, 'If you hear a noise, teach it.') It was rather that he lacked the faculty that instinctively recognises comic possibilities at every turn. A very distinguished member of the Classical Sixth recalls a Greek Testament lesson with him in which a passage was being considered that deprecated several human shortcomings, including fornication. To members of the form England seemed to be slow to deal with this important topic and one of them asked, doubtless with some *arrière pensée*, 'What about fornication, sir?' 'I'm soon coming to that,' said England. Collapse of form. A man with his experience of lively sixth-formers' mental processes should have known their capacity for pouncing on *doubles entendres*, scented danger in the question and not laid himself open to ribald reactions. On the other hand, Fr Genders speaks with genuine admiration of and gratitude for England's Greek Testament lessons. The contrast offers us the essential fact about England: he was a man whose considerable ability was inhibited from complete realisation by an awkward stiffness in human relations and a certain inflexibility of mind. Many Edwardians did not find him *simpatico* but there are others who are anxious to be thought of as 'an England man', as one of them put it.

However that may be, the move from New Street which Gilson had evaded was faced and accomplished under England. Barry's great Gothic pile had been in use for ninety-one years when he arrived and those years had seen considerable developments in education, in Birmingham and in the school itself. The fact that no classic grove secluded the hallowed New Street site may have been a cause for self-congratulation to honest Brummies but it did not facilitate the processes of education in the busy centre of the nation's 'second city'. By now the school was congested, noisy and dark. The reader will recollect that one hundred years previously the possibility of moving the school out of the centre of the city had been mooted by the governors but blocked by public opinion. Now, in the 1930s, the educational case for moving was much stronger and was recognised, not only by some of the governors, but by HM Inspectors as well. It could be opposed only by pieties which, however understandable, could not be grounded in rational argument. As one OE puts it now 'to many OEs the mere suggestion of pulling down the old school was sacrilege and when it actually happened, England got most of the blame'. To the then Bishop of Birmingham (a prominent OE, a governor of the school, a Fellow of Trinity College, Cambridge, a distinguished mathematician and amateur theologian), the destruction of Barry's building was 'an act of vandalism'.

In December 1935, when demolition was about to begin and when land for a new school had been bought three years previously, England spoke at the last OE Triennial Dinner to be held in the Big School of Barry's building. He compared himself to Daniel in the lions' den and admitted that he was 'chiefly responsible for this being the last occasion on which this dinner can take place in this magnificent room'. At this point he was interrupted by cries of 'Shame', but he went doggedly on to assert that 'it was boys and not walls that make a school' and to stress the appalling fire risks of the existing building. It was not its present situation that had ensured the school's continuing tradition of excellence and 'twenty acres of green grass would not make it impossible to win classical or any other scholarships'. To which there was really no answer.

Unlike the governors of the 1830s those a century later could be fairly sure that the Foundation was going to be able to afford a new building. The proceeds from the sale of a large site in the middle of a great city would ensure that. With land already bought some three miles from the centre of town (opposite the site of the school's playing-fields in Edgbaston) the governors invited designs for the new building and those of Mr H. W. Hobbiss, an OE, were adopted. The New Street schools had been sold and the developers were keen to press forward with demolition, so Hobbiss first had to provide temporary wooden buildings for the

The site of the present school in the early stages of construction, showing the two lodge houses on either side of what would eventually become the Foundation Office.

A view of the Temporary Buildings facing the Bristol Road. The tram lines along the central reservation were removed when trams were withdrawn in the early 1950s.

Tom Burgess (1935–51), a splendid teacher of classics and English, in action in the Temporary Buildings in the late Thirties. He moved on to become headmaster of KES, Five Ways.

two schools while the main building work went on. It was to these temporary buildings that the school decamped in January 1936. Hardly was it settled in them than, during the night of 5–6 May, by one of life's little ironies that Thomas Hardy himself could scarcely have bettered, they were totally destroyed by fire. Boys arriving for school on the morning of 6 May found only the urinals standing proud among the ashes. School work continued in the Great Hall of the neighbouring university in conditions similar to those in the Big School of previous centuries. One OE remembers, however, that his class was taught in a little room in the postgraduate department that was bafflingly nicknamed the Brewery. He found it hard to concentrate there, and recalls gradually shifting his chair round a pillar so as to be out of the sun and Maurice Porter's field of vision as the latter explained the mysteries of sines, cosines and tangents. Some classes were even taught *al fresco* but this situation did not last long. By the following September new temporary buildings had been erected and were in use, and it was in these that the work of the school continued until the outbreak of war in September 1939. The governors' response to this event was to instruct the builders to keep going even though they may have only a man and a boy on the site and it was Hobbiss's resolution and ingenuity that saw this policy through. It proved to be providential as after the war costs had risen considerably.

Like Jeune a hundred years before him England had to endure three years of his Chief Mastership in temporary buildings but that was not the end of his trials. There was in addition a year's exile at Repton. In his speech on Speech Day in December 1939, after one term of evacuation, England said, 'Of one thing evacuation has convinced me and that is the enormous – almost untapped – reservoir of common goodwill that has made this scheme work.' He went on to mention the impossibility of achieving 'a full-time, fully efficient and hard-working day school out here'. He then instanced thirteen open awards as 'a reminder of what we were like when we were in our own home'. He added that 'I have never seen the school so healthy, so cheerful and so obviously happy as

KES returns from Repton for Christmas 1939.

I have seen it this term.' Not everyone would have agreed with this patriotic assessment, and beneath the polite acknowledgements to Repton School and to the billeting authorities one sees that England was pining for Birmingham and his new baby in Edgbaston. And so was everyone else. The experiences of individual evacuees naturally varied considerably. For many rather cocky Edwardians having to conform to the routines of other people's lives was no doubt a salutary experience, and not all were as unfortunate as one who, until his mother moved him smartly home, was billeted with a local doctor who insisted that he eat meat although he was a vegetarian. Other boys had a six-mile journey each way to and from school which made getting back to a midday meal, the only hot meal of the day, something of a problem. None of the boys had the luck of some of the masters. Ted Leeds, for instance, was billeted at the Every Arms where he was only too happy to serve behind the bar. The Chief Master also found himself accommodated in a pub, the Red Lion, but there is no record of his being usefully and genially occupied in pulling a pint or two.

When the school returned after a year of what the *OE Gazette* described as the 'Reptonian captivity' enough of the new school had been built for it to be usable. Teaching began there in Septebmer 1940 although Big School, the Science Block and the Dining Hall were still in the builders' hands. Of course, life on what was still in some respects a building site was not ideal. Stacked between the school and the temporary buildings were the numbered stones of the Upper Corridor from the New Street building, awaiting reassembly as a War Memorial when time should serve. Moreover, the temporary buildings were now occupied

The return from Reptonian exile. The first term in the as yet unfinished new building in Edgbaston begins on 18 September 1940.

99

A.S. Langley, Second Master
(1934–45), Acting Chief Master
(1941–44).

by troops. Later in the war these troops were to be Americans who proved a useful source of cigarettes for Ken Tynan in his sixth-form years. He found that mentioning the date of the school's foundation was an incentive to generosity. But after only two terms in the new buildings a further disruption occurred.

For some considerable time England had been fighting against the debilitating effects of Parkinson's disease and on 1 May 1941, he had to write to Langley, now Second Master, 'I am very doubtful whether I shall be able to come to school on Tuesday next ... Unless I can get my strength back I do not think it will be possible for me to carry on.' He added that he was resigning from the end of that term. It was sad that no sooner had he settled in the building on which he had set his heart than he had to leave it. Somehow this conjunction of events distils a poignant sense of not quite fully realised potential that hangs over his career at King Edward's, deriving perhaps from a certain ridigity of mind and difficulty in relishing human contacts. But it took a courageous and determined man to bring about the move from New Street, and England's true memorial is the present school building which that move brought into existence; for although the move would no doubt have taken place sooner or later there is equally no doubt that it was England who concentrated the minds of the governors and who, in spite of unforeseen setbacks, resolutely saw it through.

As England's successor the governors appointed Charles Morris, a forty-three-year-old philosophy don from Balliol. It was the first time the Chief Mastership had gone to an Oxford man since Jeune, 107 years earlier. Even a Cambridge alumnus may feel that the change in intellectual style was overdue. But because Morris could not be released from the Ministry of Supply where he was principal assistant secretary, Langley was appointed acting headmaster. For five terms he ran the school and it was a time of some difficulty. There were many disruptive factors. The school had lost 'a large number of boys who left school in the Fifths

The school prefects of 1941–2 during the period when the Second Master, Commander Langley, was Acting Chief Master.

The East front of the school.

at the beginning of the war', as a school captain observed in July 1941, explaining why games results were poor. Many members of the Common Room had joined up and their replacements did not always find things easy. The young gentlemen gave several of the ladies who came to teach at the school an unpleasantly rough ride and one or two of the men, being expatriate Europeans, proved unintelligible. The buildings were not fully complete and bombing began more or less as soon as the school returned to Birmingham. The duties of firewatching also complicated life though these were something that boys at least were likely to enjoy even if masters did not. And casting its shadow over all was the regular news of OEs killed in action, not as numerous as in the previous war – 103 as against 254 – but a perpetual sadness to those who had known them as lively boys only a few years before.

Charles Morris was finally released by the Ministry of Supply in May 1943 to become Chief Master in fact as well as in name. Like Jeune, Morris was to be Chief Master for only a short time, five years from the time of his actual arrival, but during that time he was, like Jeune again, to achieve a major change of far-reaching consequence. He saw that the Education Act of 1944 made it possible for the Foundation to escape from the bondage of the 'deficiency grant' and to stabilise its finances. He negotiated arrangements by which King Edward's School and King Edward's High School for Girls became Direct Grant schools (schools which received capitation grants direct from the Ministry of Education) and the Foundation grammar schools became Voluntary-Aided schools (schools which were funded jointly by the local authorities, the governors and the Ministry of Education). The administrative experience that Morris had gained in his four wartime years as a top civil servant fused with an exceptional quality of mind and a civilised charm of manner to make him a brilliant negotiator. Moreover, his wartime contacts in the upper reaches of the Civil Service were

A section of the hammer beam roof of Big School being hoisted into place during building operations.

Charles Morris, Chief Master (1941–48).

invaluable when it came to persuading Ellen Wilkinson, the Minister of Education, that King Edward's School should be included on the list of Direct Grant schools which the government had already closed. In these negotiations he was absolutely invaluable, and no less successful in those with the local authority. The latter secured the right to take up 50 per cent of the places in the school as free places and consequently to retain some seats on the governing body but the school retained its own admission examination (which was competitive for all candidates) and was no longer dependent on the local authority for financial assistance. This would never have been possible without the Direct Grant and it was Morris's unique combination of qualities that alone secured that.

With the completion of the fine oak hammer-beam roof of Big School and the Science Block and Dining Hall in full working order the main task was to get the school back to full pressure of work. In the five years following the end of hostilities Morris and his successor saw to it that the intellectual vitality of the school was restored to what it had been in its best pre-war days. According to

one OE Morris taught the whole sixth form a weekly philosophy lesson. 'It wasn't', he adds, 'at all clear what we are learning but it was very interesting and certainly sent me off to university with a wish to learn more about it.' Some of us may think that to foster intellectual curiosity is just what a school with intellectual pretensions is for, even though the way we live now consigns such a view to the scrap heap of lost causes. But we can be pretty certain that Morris would also have held such a view and sought to disseminate it. The process, though, was scarcely under way when, in 1948, he was offered the vice-chancellorship of Leeds University and departed. He left to his colleagues the memory of a charming and civilised man and to his successor the responsibility of continuing and completing the task of rekindling the intellectual life of the school which his administrative skill had put on a much safer financial footing.

Field Marshal Slim accompanied by the Chief Master Charles Morris and followed by the Second Master, Langley, arrives down the drive between KES and KEHS.

103

9

Meritocracy Rules

'We class schools, you see, into four grades: Leading School, First-rate School, Good School and School. Frankly,' said Mr Levy, 'School is pretty bad.'

Evelyn Waugh: *Decline and Fall*

Oh, Edward, when you were a little boy,
I'm sure you were always getting yourself measured
To prove how you had grown since the last holidays.

T. S. Eliot: *The Cocktail Party*

SEVERAL FACTORS contribute to one's feeling that the educational climate, as it affected King Edward's and schools like it, had changed after the end of the Second World War. In the first place, a buoyant spirit had been engendered by the recent Education Act of 1944 and, in the second, as a result of having had the sharp edges rubbed off them in HM Forces, a high proportion of teachers

A Common Room photograph at the end of the War including the ladies who taught at the school during the War.

were only too aware that 'there is a world elsewhere', and this tended to relax relations between them and their pupils. However, for schools with academic pretensions, such as King Edward's, the most significant change was probably the increasingly widespread acceptance of the principle that academic ability should be the indispensable criterion of university entrance. Not that King Edward's had ever recognised any other principle of selection but this had not been an absolutely universal state of affairs, particularly with regard to Oxbridge entrance. One remembers the indignant but hardly convincing polemics of some distinguished sportsmen and others whom this alarming development did not suit. As examination results assumed an increased importance, so schools with intellectual rather than social cachet began to achieve a greater national prominence.

This tendency was strengthened by the use of a common examination, the new GCE A-level, introduced about 1950, which although conceived as a certificate of education came to be used as an instrument of selection for university entrance. As the chances of entry to Oxford and Cambridge without academic ability gradually receded A-level results, state scholarships and university scholarships became increasingly important. Although it was quite some time before anything as explicitly comparative as a Norrington Table for schools appeared, schools nevertheless began to cast a beady eye on each other's tally of Oxbridge awards and A-level results. This competitiveness, while keeping schools up to the mark, encouraged a tendency to preening and chest-beating which could be rather wearisome. It also invited the charge against some, including King Edward's, that they were merely examination factories. Just how sensitive successive Chief Masters were to this charge is evidenced by the frequency with which they denied it. At no time during the post-war decades was it actually true − as the various programmes of minority-time subjects in the sixth form and the proliferation of extra-curricular activites of all kinds testified. But it would be dishonest to overlook the clenched faces that made Common-Room meetings after a less than usually good year of Oxbridge results resemble the officers' mess at an Indian hill station when there was trouble down in the bazaar.

Tom Howarth, the successor to Morris in 1948, was the first Chief Master not to be a classical scholar. He was a historian from Cambridge, an old boy of Rugby who had taught briefly at Winchester and had had, as they say, 'a good war', having won the MC, and been one of Field Marshal Montgomery's team of whizzing young liaison officers. He radiated intellectual fizz and by temperament and ability was ideally suited to the task of galvanising the intellectual life of the school. His image was far from that of the imposing guru, much more that of a dashing young don. His touch with boys was good, relaxed yet authoritative, and his sociable and entertaining company pleased most of the Common Room. He was a master of the amusingly probing epigram which he enjoyed as much as his audience and at which he was the first to roar with laughter. He set a new style in the writing of end-of-term reports by making them amusing as well as penetrating. One such, on a boy who shall be nameless, read: 'When I try to teach him he looks at me as if I were a lunatic who should be tolerated but not encouraged.' His views were never half-hearted and usually

T.E.B. Howarth, Chief Master (1948−52).

delivered with panache and an emphatic relish of the crucially expressive words. His belief, always implicit if not actually stated, that Winchester and Rugby offered an educational model which could scarcely be improved could become tiresome after a time and it certainly made him something of an educational snob, as did his apparent unawareness of any universities besides Oxford and Cambridge. He hankered after the idea of setting up a boarding-house at King Edward's although to do so would have violated one of the Foundation's most deeply rooted traditions by weakening the link with the city. But nothing came of this and it must in fairness be added that many years later, towards the end of his life, he seems to have believed that the independent day-school was the right way forward for education. There is no doubt that after he had been in the school for a couple of years things were humming. It was, therefore, the greater pity that his Chief Mastership was soured soon after the start by his handling of an unfavourable general inspection.

HM Inspectors' report of the inspection of November 1949 was less than enthusiastic. It looked as if the chickens that had hatched on the retirement of Gilson twenty years before had come home to roost. The inspectors found that the general level of teaching was not above that prevailing in a maintained grammar school and that only two departments, Music and Art, appeared to have real distinction and that not enough Oxbridge awards were being won, though classics and science were doing well. Their comments on most individual departments gave little cause for self-congratulation. The report came as a considerable shock to the Common Room, but even more of a shock was the

Roger Dunt, senior classics master for almost all of his thirty-three years in the school (1929–62). He died suddenly, still in harness. Known, rather mysteriously, as 'The Doctor'.

fact that the Chief Master accepted most of it. As a new arrival he evidently perceived that a shake-up would be very good for all concerned. He commented in a memorandum to the governors that 'it was somewhat disturbing to be shown HM Inspectors' 1930 Report and to appreciate thereby that in twenty years ... little progress seems to be recorded, except in buildings and equipment'. As a result of this adverse report Howarth was able to bring the governors to face the fact that money would have to be spent if significant improvements were to be made, spent on improving the Library, on increasing the number of masters and on improving their salaries. He wrote to the governors that 'members of the staff have been criticised for lacking inspiration and originality and the fine edge of scholarship. Such qualities are not unconnected with a man's peace of mind and financial stability.' He reinforced the point by quoting a splendid passage from a recent address by the Educational Secretary of the Oxford Appointments Board:

> The grammar school master, and to a large extent the public school master, represent a depressed class; depressed absolutely and relatively, in mind and body ... In the old days the school master ranked socially and economically with the local doctor, the lawyer and the bank manager, but now all is changed.

Howarth added 'it seems to me as plain as a pikestaff that a man cannot be expected to expound Shakespeare, Aeschylus, or Racine, with vigour and vision and originality as well as regularly when he is at his wits' end to keep a roof over his family.'

In his memoranda to the governors Howarth was level-headed, constructive and indeed optimistic about the whole business. But this was not how he appeared to the Common Room, many of whom were upset by his acceptance after only three terms in the school of the inspectors' criticisms of their personal performances. There was a feeling that he should have fought their corner more vigorously. This loss of confidence was compounded by further complications. The inspection had been short and, it was felt, perfunctory (no physics master had been seen actually teaching); but worse was the fact that it had not been exactly *protocolaire* because the chief inspector was the father of a boy in the school. The Chief Master, it was felt, should not have allowed such a situation to occur, and the fact that, either by oversight or inexperience, he did so lost him the confidence of a minority of powerful and senior Common-Room figures.

The post-war years saw a greatly increased professionalism in the coaching of games. This was largely due to the masters in charge of cricket and rugger, J. B. Guy and T. R. Parry. Each was an outsize personality. Bernard Guy had played some first-class cricket for Kent and Warwickshire and was a legend in Midlands club cricket. He was a magnificent player and on the cricket field he could only be described as a killer. The image of him in his faded Harlequin cap (reminiscent of a more famous killer, Douglas Jardine) restlessly prowling the mid-off area or hammering his relentless way to another tigerish ton, will always remain with those who played with or against him. He was a ferocious competitor with an enormous technical knowledge of all aspects of the game. He would bowl all the afternoon in the nets at members of the eleven and when they had to bowl at him he played them as concentratedly and as mercilessly as

Bernard Guy, Head of Chemistry and finally Science supremo, caught during the luncheon interval at school some years after he had ceased to terrorise all bowlers in Midlands club cricket.

The house prefects of 1953–4. Fourth from the left in the back row is Alan Smith, now Chief Executive of the TCCB.

P.B. Jackson, international rugby winger.

if he were playing an important innings. The boy who very occasionally managed to induce a false stroke felt pretty good. Guy was enormously helped by Dudley Cockle, the professional coach, who in addition to being a fine and knowledgeable player, had a marvellous touch with boys of all ages and took the eleven-year-olds as seriously as members of the eleven. Throughout the 1950s they produced between them some fine elevens in which such future first-class cricketers as O. S. Wheatley and A. C. Smith by no means eclipsed their team-mates. Full of years and gravity, these two now constitute a King Edward's mafia in the inner counsels of the game at Lords. On them, as on all members of his elevens, Guy had a profound influence; it was scarcely less on the countless boys whom he regularly propelled to an A grade in A-level chemistry.

'Bob' Parry, a pre-war Cambridge rugger blue, came from South Wales and was steeped in the game. As a coach he had the priceless gift of making the team want to work for him. When taking a rugger practice he wore the longest rugger shorts ever beheld by human eye and on one such occasion his richly Welsh accents were heard to inform a beefy character who was heaving away on the scrum machine, 'You've got a fine pair of buttocks there, boy! Now, go on, shove.' On another occasion he steamed up alongside a very fast winger who was going flat out saying 'Go on, now! Faster! Faster!' When watching the first fifteen he would isolate himself from all other spectators, enveloped in a brooding concentration that recorded every move of the ninety minutes' play for analysis at the next team meeting or practice. One of his protégés, Peter Jackson, subsequently played for England but his finest hour was probably when the school won the Public Schools Sevens at Rosslyn Park in 1956. He was also an enormously effective teacher of middle-school English. To this job he brought a splendid voice and a wealth of experience as a chief examiner in O-level English Language for the JMB which, among other things, enabled him to keep his colleagues in the department on the right lines. At parties, the moment when he took off his jacket and rolled up his sleeves to reveal awe-inspiring forearms was a signal that his characteristic mood of mildly sardonic pessimism was temporarily in abeyance and that a hilarious ebullience would ensue.

Towards the end of Howarth's time at the school normal routine was enlivened by the Great Bomb Plot. Its first manifestation was an explosion in the small filing-cabinet which Ralph Crow, the head of English, kept on his desk. It took the eyebrows off the luckless lad who kept it in order for him. This was followed by similar explosions in the Library, the Orderly Room and the Chief Master's desk in his study, the latter accompanied by a note saying 'I bet you didn't expect to find one here' – or words to that effect. All explosions were set off by the opening of a drawer and scientists reported that the triggering mechanism was most ingenious. Those investigating these outrages suspected, for reasons never made fully clear, that the next one would occur in the area of the gymnasium and so a trap was set. Craddock, one of the porters, was concealed inside a vaulting-box and left to peer through the apertures at each end of the box, and from this concealment to identify the culprit. This subtle scheme produced no result. The bomber was never discovered and the explosions just stopped, leaving a mystery as impenetrable as that of the *Marie Celeste*.

Tom Howarth's Common Room of 1951. Roberts, Jackson, Power, Ballance, and Copland, respectively fifth, sixth, seventh, tenth and eleventh from the left in the front row, were all survivors from Cary Gilson's days.

Tom Howarth's announcement to the Common Room in the early summer of 1951 that he intended to resign and return to Winchester as Master-in-College came as a bolt from the blue. He had communicated this decision to the governors the previous February before he had completed three years at the school. Both the OE Association and 300 parents wrote to urge the governors to seek to remove the difficulties which had contributed to his decision. Apart from domestic and personal reasons which, of course, were outside the area of discussion, there were two main issues. The first was Howarth's conviction that the connection with the Foundation grammar schools was injurious to the Direct Grant schools and the second was that it was impossible for one man to discharge properly the duties of head of the Foundation at the same time as being a successful Chief Master of King Edward's School. The governors could not accept the validity of either of these points and could not therefore 'remove the difficulties'. His departure was a sad loss and one cannot help but feel that perhaps his time with Montgomery, when he had the ear and the confidence of a man who could make almost anything happen, had not been the best preparation for command in the more humdrum world of educational politics.

Ronald Lunt, Chief Master (1952–74).

If Tom Howarth's resignation had come as a shock it was nothing compared to the shock of his successor. The Revd R. G. Lunt was beyond the experience of most people connected with King Edward's School, boys, parents, masters and governors alike. His credentials were daunting – an Old Etonian, a first in Greats, a chaplain in the Coldstream Guards, the SAS and the Airborne Division and, like Howarth, an MC. More important, he was an experienced headmaster, having spent six and a half years as headmaster of Liverpool College. But it was none of these facts which sent masters tottering from the first Common Room meeting; it was the new Chief Master's vocabulary and voice. The vocabulary was laced with words used slightly pedantically in their original latinate sense and, at the same time, with rather old-fashioned prep school slang plus more than a few superlatives ('how quite splendid', 'how perfectly first-class'). The voice was rich with pre-1914 vowels and very heavily stressed consonants. A rising intonation at the end of phrases created a forceful and challenging emphasis which ensured that nobody was taken in when he said, self-deprecatingly, that for a

Members of the Cartland Club photographed in the Cartland Room in its early and still civilised days.

term or two he was 'just another new boy in the place'. From the start the model was obvious – the great clerical Chief Masters of the previous century. The guru had returned.

Ronald Lunt was to rule King Edward's School for twenty-two years, from 1952 until 1974. When he arrived the governors' purposes appear to have been to achieve some measure of stability and with it to re-establish the intellectual eminence of the school. They were also anxious to develop the site. Action to achieve the latter purpose began without delay. Over the following few years the open-air swimming-bath and its accessory buildings were completed, as was the conversion of the re-erected Upper Corridor from the New Street building to a War Memorial chapel. The Cartland Corridor, comprising a large common room and five smaller rooms, was added over the classical classrooms. Unfortunately, the common room was not nearly large enough to be a general sixth-form common room and consequently it became the HQ of the newly founded Cartland Club. Election to this body was guaranteed to Oxbridge award winners, prefects, captains of games and housemasters' nominees. It was not a good idea. From the start it was perceived to be divisive and one of its first-generation members, writing from the sobriety of middle age, recorded that 'When I look back on that nefarious bloody institution it makes me cringe.' Certain rebellious spirits in the Common Room referred to it disrespectfully as 'the poor man's Pop.' It remained a contentious and increasingly discredited fact of life until its dissolution a few years ago.

Other building projects were to follow during the period of the Luntine ascendancy. Some were small-scale operations such as building a house for the Second Master, Mayo House (1957), and a new one for the Chief Master, Vince House (1959), and a scout hut (1962), whereas others were more ambitious and, perhaps, closer to the school's essential purpose. The old temporary buildings which had been used since the war by the university were demolished and the whole of the South Field was levelled, thereby considerably increasing the playing area (1961); a fine new pavilion was built on the Eastern Road playing-field along with an all-weather running track (1963); a Music School and a Language Laboratory was added (1965); the Art and Design Department was enlarged (1970) and a large sports hall with squash courts and facilities for indoor cricket nets was built, largely the gift of parents through the KES Fund (1971). Overall these years saw a good deal added to the school plant.

The year of Ronald Lunt's arrival was the school's quatercentenary year. A royal visit had been planned but the death of the king in February meant that this had to be postponed. It finally took place in 1955. The visit was scheduled for November so as soon as the autumn term began the school, in conjunction with its next-door neighbours at KE High School, embarked on a rehearsal programme which seemed to rival that for the Normandy landings. In spite of this there was, on the Great Day, a very slight hitch in the proceedings in Big School which led the present writer to the following epigram:

> Our gracious queen was here today,
> Dropped in as she was passing;
> Her call was so informal that
> She caught us still rehearsing.

A group of Cartland Club members (1954–55) centred on the imposing figure of Henry Craddock, holding instead of the more conventional rugger ball the ceremonial communal teapot.

111

It was, nevertheless, a great day for the school and, of course, not without its lighter moments. At one point the Queen was complimenting a boy on a beautiful wood carving that he had made and asked what wood he had used. 'It's yew, ma'am', he answered, only to realise immediately the possible pun and to turn appropriately crimson. The Queen made a graceful reply which made it clear that she knew what he meant and enabled him to retire in good order. A moment fraught with disastrous potential occurred when Her Majesty left. The police had decided that she should leave by the back way which necessitated her car passing a large heap of coke. As this was a considerable eyesore it was decreed that it should be hidden by swarms of loyal boys standing on and in front of it, in the charge of two masters in full academicals leading the cheers. This was certainly one better than painting it white which, as legend has it, is said to occur in such cases at military establishments. The trouble was, however, that a ten-foot-high coke heap offers no stable footing and there was much sliding and slithering. It was only by the mercy of God that boys and masters did not find themselves in a tangled heap in front of the royal car as it approached.

The Queen's visit 1955. Her Majesty and Chief Master Lunt discuss the model of The Queen's Beast, constructed by Roger Harper who stands proprietorially by. The model is now permanently in the school library.

PLATE 5 'The Nativity' – a design for stained glass by Sir Edward Burne-Jones Bt (1833 – 98). He was a pupil at the school during Gifford's Chief Mastership.

PLATE 6   A recent watercolour of St Philip's Church by J.L.S. Surman. On the creation of the Diocese of Birmingham in 1905 the church became Birmingham Cathedral.

The Queen's visit, 1955. The School Captain, Roger Wilson, presents Her Majesty with a copy of T.W. Hutton's History of King Edward's School.

At the end of his first term the new Chief Master had appointed as head of science Dr Harold Mayor, who became one of the school's greatest assets, presiding as he did over its most consistently brilliant department. At the same time he promoted the present writer to become head of the English department in which he had been teaching for a couple of years. For the rest of Lunt's time at the school the only changes at head-of-department level were occasioned by the sad death of Roger Dunt, the head of classics, in 1961 and the retirement of E. V. Smith, the Second Master and head of mathematics, in 1970. All three posts were filled within the school, Eric Williams, the school chaplain, becoming head of classics, Peter Chapman becoming head of maths and Harold Mayor becoming Second Master. And when, in 1973, Eric Williams retired to become Vicar of Barnt Green his job as head of classics was again filled from within the school by Martin Tennick. Lunt was a great believer in internal promotions, although nowadays this is a decidedly unfashionable policy on the quite unproven supposition that it makes for stagnation.

H.A. Mayor, head of science (1952–76), Second Master (1970–76).

Such was the inescapable ambience of the Chief Master's personality that it is easy to overlook others, strong personalities themselves, who did much to determine the tone of the school during the 1950s and 1960s. Such were Jim Biggs and Charles Blount, heads of the modern languages and history departments respectively, both influential and colourful figures, the penetration of whose voices was unrivalled until John Hatton arrived in the mid-1960s to set quite new standards of decibel power. Biggs, a brilliant linguist as might be expected in a disciple of the legendary Acatos, was a very influential figure, almost an *éminence grise*. He was deeply devoted to King Edward's, yet such was his complex personality that he habitually masked his feelings behind a distancing irony that suggested a degree of scepticism which did not really exist. There was no such strategy in Blount's statement of views. He was the most direct of men

A school party to Armagnac country detrains at (probably) Agen. Ted Leeds and Jim Biggs (in profile wearing the famous Beret Basque) are to be seen centre stage. School caps were apparently still *de rigeur* in deepest Gascony.

and his manner the most positive. It was his plonking certainty backed up by his mastery of a wealth of detail that delighted most of the boys whom he taught. He was not an admirer of A. J. P. Taylor and the Common Room echoed for days to his delight when a misprint in a weekly periodical described the latter as 'the well-known shitorian'. He refused to believe that it was a printing error.

Another forceful character was the school's *kapellmeister*, Dr Willis Grant. He was a Mancunian, ebullient and robust, a sensitive musician and very fine organist. He had a keen eye for the comic and grotesque and these qualities characterised most of his anecdotes which were usually prefaced with a faintly conspiratorial 'You'll never believe this ...' He made boys want to sing for him and was a much sought-after organ-teacher both within and without the school. As a result a succession of Edwardians won organ scholarships to Oxbridge. How was it, then, that with so able and winning a personality in charge music did not make a much bigger impact in the school?

114

The answer is in the thoroughly misguided tradition that linked the post of master in charge of music with that of cathedral organist. It was a totally unsatisfactory arrangement; it meant that the music master was inevitably a church musician – not necessarily the best qualification for the job – and, moreover, that he could only devote half his time and energy to it. As a result of the system, David Munrow, a boy who arguably had a more powerful combination of talent and dynamism than any other Edwardian of the post-war period, had to create the context for his colossal musical energies. He was a bassoonist, not an organist, was not taking A-level music and as there was no regular school orchestra he could not come within the orbit of Dr Grant's teaching. But with the latter's encouragement he galvanised boys and masters who played an instrument into giving recitals and chamber concerts; his enormous talents were not only musical but entrepreneurial. He was lucky in that the Common Room at that time had some excellent instrumental players: Norman Craig, Bill Barlow, Jim Bolton and Chris Dodds and two excellent keyboard players, Eric Williams and Ronnie Allison. Munrow was a phenomenon who would have made things hum whatever the circumstances and the absence of a full range of formally organised musical opportunities did him no harm. But for more run-of-the-mill instrumentalists the absence of orchestral opportunities was sad. It was Tim Tunnard, Willis Grant's successor, who took the vital step of starting a joint orchestra with the girls from the High School next door. It was a very important development and the foundation from which the really first-class orchestras of later years could grow. When the link with the cathedral was finally broken in the mid-1970s and two full-time music masters, Gordon Sill and Peter Bridle, were appointed school music really took off. A first and second orchestra, a concert band, a brass group and a jazz group are now in regular action.

A contemporary of David Munrow who also became nationally known is Bill Oddie and perhaps it would be well to put the record straight about his schooldays. Widespread legend has it that when at school Bill was a wild and anarchic figure, the moving spirit behind such merry pranks as directing traffic off Edgbaston Park Road and down the school drive. The truth is less colourful. He was certainly a great entertainer on the coach going to and from away fixtures with the first fifteen, but in all important respects he was a pillar of the establishment – a member of the first fifteen, captain of his house, school prefect and exhibitioner in English at Pembroke College, Cambridge, a model pupil in fact. He wrote the script of a good revue which was, sadly, almost the last in a sequence of such entertainments that flourished in the late 1950s. The Chief Master wrote on one of his reports 'If he thinks he can make a living by making people laugh, he is much mistaken.' We all make mistakes.

In 1963 HM Inspectors exorcised the spectres of 1949. They reported that the Chief Master and his staff could take considerable satisfaction in the progress made since the previous inspection. Their report came in the middle of two decades of important developments. The fact that the school now had a chapel, a clerical Chief Master and a chaplain meant that Holy Communion could be regularly celebrated and evensong regularly said or sung. It also led to the

A scene from *Murder in the Cathedral* (1954). John Pettitt as the Second Templer and John Grimley Evans as Becket.

A scene from James Bolton's 1966 production of *Othello*. This was the last production in which boys played girls' parts. Kevin Lee (seated) played Desdemona and is now a professional actor and dramatist. He won the Writers' Guild Award in 1991.

formation under Dr Grant of a small, specialised chapel choir to sing evensong unaccompanied. It was also in this period that the school chaplain, Eric Williams, and one of his colleagues in the classical department created the Personal Service Group which worked every Friday afternoon in deprived areas, principally Balsall Heath. The organisation of this work was carried on by subsequent chaplains, Michael Gudgeon, Robert Grimley and Richard Crocker and later by another member of the classical department, Robert Tibbott.

Considerable expansion also took place in several departments, in art and craftwork, in drama and physical education. The foundations of these departmental expansions had been laid earlier with Morris's appointment of Bruce Hurn to the art department and Howarth's appointment of Ralph Crow to the English department. For twenty-five years Hurn was to run a dynamic department that produced a great variety of interesting and talented work and was to go on doing so after he had been called to higher things in the inspectorate. A major creative effort for which he was responsible was furnishing the chapel. For several years teams of enthusiasts from the craft department laboured away under his direction, making pews and benches for the chapel, carving the pew-ends, constructing and carving the clergy stalls and painting the roof-bosses. Hurn himself painted a large crucifixion to serve as a reredos to the altar. It was a fine, sustained team-effort.

As for drama, Crow was never happy unless he was directing a play and he soon instituted a yearly junior play to keep himself occupied after the senior play had been produced. Soon after he left in 1952 an end-of-the-year play was introduced into the calendar as well, making three regular productions each year. The range of plays chosen for production was considerably widened. A three-year cycle was evolved for the senior play in which a play by Shakespeare, a non-Shakespearian classic and a modern play alternated. The 1950s and 1960s saw some excellent productions but the school exhibited a curiously ambivalent

A scene from *The Second Shepherd's Play* (1959). Actors from left to right are Rodney Braithwaite, Tony Moreton, Peter Cairns, Alistair Papps and David Munrow.

attitude towards them. They were fine so long as they didn't get in the way. They were applauded and often enjoyed by large numbers of people; they were reviewed favourably in the *Birmingham Post*; but a house rugger match was often deemed to constitute a more urgent claim on a boy's time than a dress rehearsal. In 1965 a production of T. S. Eliot's *The Family Reunion* to mark its author's death which had occurred early in the year was the first production in which girls from KEHS took part, a quantum leap in the cause of school drama as it greatly extended the range of possible plays. It was the seed from which a joint dramatic society with KEHS was to grow. In 1968 an Old Edwardian, Michael Parslew, took over the drama. Immediately the scale of operations was vastly extended. The new Joint Dramatic Society took productions to Falmouth, to the fringe at the Edinburgh Festival and to Germany, playing in Frankfurt and West Berlin. It developed a combination of military discipline and holy zeal to equal that of the Knights Templar in their early, uncorrupted days. Parslew's productions, if a touch cerebral, were excellent and during his directorate the JDS was certainly the thing to be in.

John Pendry's design for the programme cover of the 1955 production of Jonson's *The Alchemist.*

The arrival of Keith Symes in the late 1950s gave much greater prominence to all aspects of physical education. He was a man with a mission and everything about him, from his walk to his talk, radiated energy and vitality. He and John Cotter, invaluable anchor-man of the department, proved a most effective combination. When it was further strengthened by the arrival of Derek Everest and later Stuart Birch, both of whom succeeded in the fullness of time to its command, things were really humming. Gradually throughout the period the range of available games was widened. In addition to the time-hallowed cricket, rugger, fives, athletics and swimming, hockey was introduced and with the building of a games hall in 1971 squash. The arrival of Brian Tomlinson to teach modern languages in 1965 gave a tremendous fillip to tennis in the school and was to produce some high-class players in subsequent years.

Because of its site immediately opposite the university the school was ideally placed for infiltration during the heady days of student power during the 1960s. Considering this, it remained remarkably stable thoughout the ferment of those years. Occasionally a whiff of the siege of Lucknow scented the air, as when a proposed visit from Enoch Powell to address a school society had to be cancelled because the university authorities warned that the students had planned a reception for him. This brought a notice from the Chief Master explaining the cancellation and ending with the ringing sentiments 'A sad, bad day for all of us. I do not recall being so cast down since the fall of Tobruk.' (It may be mentioned that at that time Lunt himself had fallen, temporarily, into the hands of the enemy.) Of course, it was not an easy time. Anti-authority impulses were in the air and the chaps were understandably excited by them. Within the classroom pressures to substitute endless circular discussions for teaching and learning were strong. Because of his position and large-scale personality the Chief Master became the target of rebellious feelings. But attempts by roving missionaries from the university to extend the doctrine of student power by making King Edward's a bastion of pupil power were notably ineffective. This was partly because, when the chips were down, the boys were fundamentally

Action in the Fives courts before they were roofed over.

interested in their work, and partly because the Chief Master kept his head and did nothing to create a focal point for the vaguely discontented feelings that were abroad in the school. This was most strikingly evident in his refusal to be noticeably interested in the then-contentious matter of long hair, though one suspects that he was under some pressure to do something about it. Some boys looked as elegant and well groomed as Caroline courtiers, some looked a ghastly mess and some just looked dotty. But it was clearly a matter of no essential importance whatever; Lunt's avoidance of the kind of silly public splutterings on the subject by which, at that time, many a headmaster made a fool of himself was a major factor in avoiding challenges to order within the school. So although it was harder to keep the boys concentrated there were no confrontations. And considering again the proximity of the university and the proselytising tendency of the drug culture, there was mercifully no real drug problem, to everyone's great relief. Compared with the disruption in some schools King Edward's came through the period relatively painlessly.

Somewhere about 1970 occurred the Case of the Phantom Sixth-Former. A temporary master – who shall be called X – came to teach modern languages for a term. When he took the names of the boys in his Divisions set they told him that one boy was absent, a certain A. N. Once. After a few periods, at none

In 1973 not even the Senior Service could clip the 'lokkes crulle' of swinging youth. A distinctly period piece.

of which Once appeared, X asked if he were still absent. Yes, he was told, but Once would be back next week. The following week the boys in the set briefed a crony, who happened to have a private-study period and so was available to assume the mantle of Once, to turn up to impersonate him. Once was missing again the following period – no convenient private-study period allowing the impersonator to be free to pursue his act – but his prep was produced which, it was said, he had sent in by a friend but which the form had carefully manufactured themselves. Once would be back as soon as his health allowed. And so, unbelievably, it went on to the end of term. Once made fleeting appearances whenever the timetable allowed and was even impersonated by different characters; but his appearances were so few and the gaps between them so long that when someone claiming to be Once did turn up the dazed X had forgotten what he had looked like the time before.

Life with Canon Lunt – for so he had become – was often bumpy and safety-belts needed to be permanently fastened. When he retired in 1974 those of us who had been in the trenches throughout the whole campaign were disconcerted by the eerie quiet that followed. He had been Chief Master for twenty-two years, the first Chief Master since Gilson to last more than twenty and, along with Gilson and Vardy, the only one since Cooke to do so. Throughout the entire period he had, like Vardy, worked all hours of the day and night for the school. Over such a period a degree of identification of master and school can develop which is not really possible in a shorter span. It is no exaggeration to say that King Edward's School was the love of Canon Lunt's life. But his relationship with his beloved was not easy. His manner was of one born to the purple, masterful and autocratic, often abrasive and domineering and most people were at one time or another enraged by him. He did not conceal his disagreements or his disapproval and to survive in his school you had to be both able and tough; for those who weren't, masters or boys, life was a distinct trial. Most masters devised their own strategies for survival and once one was accustomed to an occasional, sudden bombardment (often several sheets of foolscap typed in single-spacing announcing that the Chief Master was 'shocked and grieved' about something one had failed to do and often prefaced by a quotation from Aristotle) life was certainly earnest and stimulating. The long monologues of Common Room meetings were only lightened by the high-pitched whirr of J. D. Copland's hearing-aid when he decided that he had had enough and switched it off.

Lunt had a true understanding of intellectual life, set a true value on it and sought to foster it in every way. It was this that led him to make large-scale prize essays obligatory for all sixth-formers and to create complicated schemes to occupy them after the A-level examinations. If the schemes were rather too elaborate and labour-intensive the intention was right; some of the prize essays done by post-Oxbridge candidates over a couple of terms were genuinely scholarly and much excellent drama and music was performed by the post-A-level boys. Lunt started three play-reading societies, one for Shakespeare, one for other Elizabethan dramatists and one for Greek drama, and a Common Room discussion group which he rather bafflingly called the Commune. If both boys

John Hodges, teacher of French and Spanish (1950–84) and Second Master (1976–81).

As the post of Usher gave place to that of Second Master so Second Master gave place to Deputy Chief Master. Roger Skinner was the last of the Second Masters, holding that honourable position from 1981–88.

and masters became irritated by the frequently barked rhetorical question at Big School prayers, 'What are we here for?' the answers, which the Chief Master did not stay for but hastened to supply himself, were always on the side of the angels, to wit, 'good learning' and an understanding of the concepts of service and what he called a 'fair-do', i.e. justice. In an increasingly anti-intellectual and materialist world these points could not be made too often. On the whole he was good with boys who were in trouble outside school and supportive of those who suffered with inadequate or unjust parents. Moreover, as he showed when he took over the Latin in a fifth form whose master left at Christmas, he was an excellent classroom teacher.

However lordly his manner may have been it certainly enabled him to produce some very good one-liners. His report to the Common Room of a visit to the War Office to state the case for the school Cadet Corps is a case in point. Having deployed his arguments with irresistible cogency he delivered his parting shot at the bemused brigadier whom he had been to see – 'Well, general, it's your battle now'. He did not say which of his ties, Old Etonian, Airborne Division or Brigade of Guards he wore to soften up the opposition. Perhaps it was his clerical collar. On another occasion the headmistress of KE High School was describing with unstoppable unction the indignation felt by one of her prefects who had overheard the parent of a junior girl being beastly to her daughter. When Lunt finally managed to get a word in – an unfamiliar situation for him – it was perfect. 'Well, Miss Lloyd-Williams, I must say you've got some pretty prim gals in that school of yours.' Even if managers and company secretaries had not in recent years begun to furnish the personality model for headmasters we could safely say that we should not look upon his like again and the loss to education is considerable. He was, to use one of his favourite phrases, *sui generis*.

Canon Lunt's last year or two was overcast with the possibility of the withdrawal of the Direct Grant in the event of a Labour election victory. In a paper which he read in December 1972 to the Commune he foresaw clearly that the Direct Grant would 'die within the decade'. By the time he actually went in July 1974 the government had changed and the loss of the Direct Grant was much more imminent.

It was left to his successor, Robson Fisher, to help the governors to deal with this situation. It would be difficult to imagine a stronger contrast than that between him and Lunt. If Lunt had marked the return of the guru Fisher marked the advent of the mandarin. He had read Honour Mods and English at Oxford, had been headmaster of Bryanston School for thirteen years and was quiet, self-effacing, modest in manner but, as time would reveal, often unexpectedly tough in action. He was aware when he first came to King Edward's of what he has called the 'rather ridiculous awe' in which the Chief Master was held in Birmingham.

Whatever may have been the case in the past general feeling about the school in the city during the post-war period makes an interesting study. For about thirty years it has been possible to take opposed views of it on strictly political grounds and when one considers its history there is nothing new about that. But

Robson Fisher, Chief Master (1974–82).

120

because only a tiny fraction of Birmingham's large population has first-hand knowledge of it, public perception of the school is largely a matter of myth, like people's perception of what life is like in a monastery or a palace. Several myths are current: that it is a rarefied, intellectual hothouse that has to be spoken of in tones of awe-struck wonder; that a boy who gains admission is automatically brilliant; that it is a snooty establishment reserved for the privileged; that it is a reactionary dump; and so on. Needless to say there is little basis of fact in any of these ideas any more than in the complementary myth held by some Old Edwardians, that it is the finest school in the country. The school of which that can be said does not, of course, exist.

Fisher's first reaction to life in the school itself was that the tension which Lunt's forcefulness had created needed to be relaxed. He quickly took an important and symbolic step in this direction by removing the prefects from their adversarial station facing the rest of the boys in Big School, like a row of minders between the *capo mafia* and those out to fix him. Fisher felt that it was impossible to conduct school prayers in that atmosphere and so had the prefects sitting down and facing the front like everyone else. He also encouraged masters to conduct the proceedings while he sat among the *hoi polloi*. He has said that when he arrived at King Edward's he found the sixth form socially awkward though very clever and the place as a whole much saner than Bryanston because it is a day-school and everybody goes home at night. Another consequence of this, however, was that he also felt a distinct lack of a sense of community whereas Lunt, on his arrival, had felt a strong sense of tradition. Like many headmasters Fisher was anxious to teach some senior boys but unlike some he made sure that he taught the junior boys as well. He achieved this by teaching each third-year form four periods per week for half a term. This meant that after a few years he had taught, albeit briefly, every boy in the school. A former head-mistress of KEHS, Dr Smith, had initiated a similar scheme twenty-five years earlier.

On 26 February 1975, the governors noted that from September 1976, the government intended to phase out the Direct Grant and recorded their intention 'to continue to keep King Edward's School and King Edward's High School for Girls accessible to academically able children and, by offering some free and assisted places to pupils whose parents have only limited means, to ensure that no suitable pupil is denied admission to these schools solely on financial grounds'. From this decision grew a complicated system of financial help for such pupils who entered the school from 1976 onwards, provided at first by the Foundation itself and later by the government's Assisted Places Scheme; between them, they ensured that the governors' intention of 1975 has been achieved. In the evolution of both these schemes Fisher played a conspicuous part and there is no doubt that the enforced change to independent status was the biggest challenge that the school faced during his Chief Mastership. In prospect, this change seemed to be not without hazard. It looked as though the number of entrance candidates might well be reduced and consequently the calibre of entrants might drop because the head teachers of some primary schools, as a matter of policy and conviction, turned King Edward's face to the wall and withheld information

The author in action at a rehearsal of *The Playboy of the Western World*, the end-of-the-year play in 1978.

about the school from their pupils. But in the event the transition to independence proceeded smoothly enough, partly because of the financial provisions already mentioned but even more because of the reputation and considerable momentum that the school had developed during its years as a Direct Grant school. The change to independence has, however, probably produced a more solidly middle- and professional-class entry which is not something to be unreservedly pleased about.

A very different kind of development that began at the same time as these changes of status was the appointment of Mrs Eileen Worthington to teach geography. Its importance can scarcely be exaggerated. Mrs Worthington was the first woman teacher to be appointed on a permanent basis to King Edward's School and although she did not herself stay for long she blazed a trail along which other women have followed. They have all made (and are making) a great contribution to the school in many ways beyond the sheer success and excellence of their classroom teaching. They have had a tonic influence well in excess of their numbers and it would be good to see more of them. It is particularly salutary that clever boys should be confronted by women who are just as clever and know a good deal more than they do. Scarcely less so is the fact that the Common Room can no longer be quite as cosily dominated by undiluted male assumptions.

Robson Fisher's Chief Mastership is tangibly commemorated by the new biology and computing block that was conceived and initiated during his time at the school and which is named after him. In 1982 he resigned to take up a post as Deputy Secretary to the Headmasters' Conference and to the Secondary Heads' Association. He was followed in office at King Edward's by Martin Rogers. The new Chief Master came to King Edward's after eleven years as headmaster of Malvern College. He was another Cambridge product with a mixed degree in Natural Sciences and History, a fact which suggests that he valued knowledge in a different way from his predecessors. There was a strong contrast with Fisher in style and manner. Dark-suited and striped-shirted, as opposed to Fisher who was light-suited and plain-shirted, Rogers never

Work in primary schools has been a main activity of the Personal Service Group. *Below:* Robert Tibbott, who did so much for PS, is seen with another member of the group on a Friday afternoon assignment in an inner city school. *Below right:* Robert Tibbot dispatches two Personal Service workers to their Friday assignment before doing the rounds himself.

suggested the don, the guru or the mandarin; he was incarnate chief executive. From the start he aimed at big changes and it is a tribute to his single-mindedness and determination that he carried them all through in the space of nine years – whether people liked them or not. The fundamental perceptions behind his development plan were that the school needed to expand, in numbers and in outlook, and that it should be more firmly hitched (as he saw it, squeaking) to the wagon of enterprise and technology.

To achieve the first of these objectives the annual intake was increased from a four-form to a five-form entry which, over a period of seven years from 1987, would increase the number from 680 to about 850. Inevitably this entailed providing more classroom space and so the creation of more classrooms became the starting-point of a much larger building programme. The changing-rooms on the South Front became the new classrooms and extensive new changing-rooms were added to the swimming-pool area while the pool itself was roofed and enlarged. The construction of a Design Centre, an entirely new building purpose-built to house an entirely new subject, Craft, Design and Technology, released for alternative use the rooms that had previously constituted the Art Department. The expansion of the school also entailed an increase in the numbers of masters and this in turn necessitated a new and larger Masters' Common Room. In addition to these large-scale developments that were the core of the Grand Design changes on a smaller scale were made. The badly planned area just inside the main door to the school has been much altered. The locker room, strikingly unattractive and appallingly placed so as to be the first thing seen on entering the building, has been converted into a small bookshop and a much-needed large drama studio. Giles Evans, who was in charge of drama at the time

Above: Valerie Shipway (1980–88) and *Opposite top:* Kate Barnett (1980–86) taught, respectively, modern languages and English with great flair and success. Their presence was a great tonic to the school.

The Design Centre, opened in the school year 1989–90.

The RN section of the CCF visit HMS Dolphin, October 1985. The Lieutenant in charge is Martin Stead who has followed Derek Benson as master i/c cricket.

Martin Rogers, Chief Master (1982–91) and chairman of HMC in 1987.

of the conversion, brooded, agonised and watched over its design and construction, and it was right that after his tragically early death a few years later he should be commemorated by a plaque on its inner wall. The area by the porters' lodge has been refurbished with the entirely laudable aim of giving a touch of style to the depressingly undistinguished entry which the architect had created. Whether the result is as successful as the intention was right is far from certain; some may find the designs on the glass fussy.

The Grand Design was not, however, confined to buildings; indeed, buildings were a consequence rather than the heart of it. In the first place, it envisaged developing closer links with industry and to that end Jack Jenkins was appointed as Industrial Fellow, his salary paid by Barclays Bank, to teach a half timetable of economics and to promote much closer contact between boys and industrial management. In the second place it involved what, in the trendy jargon of the Church of England, is called 'outreach'. The aim was to extend the benefit of what King Edward's has to offer to children below the normal age of entry. The Project for Gifted Children is a scheme whereby the school arranges Saturday courses for clever children outside the school. These courses are taught largely by members of staff and take place in several of the Foundation schools. The whole project was funded initially by the Dulverton Trust, the Grantham Yorke Trust and the governors, and John Evans was appointed to be its first director and in addition to teach a half timetable of classics and general studies. Another initiative was the institution of leadership courses and these were organised and supervised by Ken Jones, a member of the maths department.

Then there was the matter of the curriculum. Lunt had introduced economics and Fisher computing and Rogers was to be the apostle of Design. The two curriculum reviews during his era led to adjustments in the arrangements for teaching modern languages (a subject to which he rightly attached great importance), to increasing the importance of geography by equalising its position in the timetable with that of history, and to making way for CDT. To accommodate the latter subject a large and expensive new building (the Martin Rogers Design Centre) rose up from the tennis-courts at the end of the main drive, financed partly from funds and partly by an appeal which raised over a million pounds from industry, parents and old boys. This very large-scale development preoccupied Rogers during the final years of his Chief Mastership and there is reason to believe that when he dies Design will be found written in his heart.

These were not the only changes to quicken the pulses during Rogers's Chief Mastership. One fruitful development has been to create strong links with the Collège S. Marc in Lyons and with the Gutenbergschule in Wiesbaden. Others, generated partly externally and partly internally, have tended to enlarge the bureaucratic component in the life of the school. In the first place, the introduction of the new GCSE examination and the need to make sure that the objectives of the National Curriculum are being met has increased masters' clerical burden. In the second place, the creation of a Management Committee to augment the august hierarchies of housemasters and heads of departments, has increased the opportunities for meetings. The chain of command, too, has been

Konzertmeister Peter Bridle rehearses the First Orchestra (now called the KES Symphony Orchestra) in Big School, 1983.

significantly altered by the replacement of the Second Master by a Deputy Head, a post that has been splendidly filled by the former head of history, David Buttress. There is no doubt that these initiatives have made a deep impact on the school and they have been accompanied by a change in the way that the school presents itself to the world. It now sees itself in a competitive market and, in spite of its known excellence, devotes much more time and energy to public relations. They have also produced a change of tone within the school which reflects changing national perceptions of what education should be aiming at. National perceptions are not, of course, always right and this makes it likely that some of the recent changes will have a more permanent value than others. Rogers is the first to admit that only time will tell how successful they have been.

Nevertheless, while they have been taking place the school has been achieving outstanding results at what it is really good at, to wit, academic work. At the same time extra-curricular activity has flourished – games, rugger tours, expeditions, camps, foreign trips and so on. The First Orchestra takes Shostakovich in its stride and has had a rehearsal taken by Simon Rattle, and the Dramatic Society has plunged into musicals. Equally lively have been the school's multifarious societies, nearly all of them having been for some years run jointly with KE High School. 'Particular friendships' between the 'yonge, fresshe folkes, he or she' are no longer regarded as evidence of dangerous depravity; indeed, in the sixth forms some subjects which attract relatively few customers are even taught jointly, a process which began with Greek in the late 1960s. And so close is the *entente cordiale* that on a recent Red Nose Day one of the boys passed the whole morning in class at KE High School dressed as a girl while one of the girls, in boy's school uniform, did the same at the boys' school.

David Buttress, OE, a splendid Head of the History Department (1975–8) and then first Deputy Chief Master (1988–), here seen in 1981 taking his ease with a biscuit and a cup of tea.

The Junior Challenge team of 1984. Left to right: Martin Potter, Dougal McCrow, Christopher Nash, Phillip Blenkinsop and Matthew Grimley.

Not all meetings of the Shakespeare Society end like this in the garden of the Sun Barrels. But the photograph offers a fine illustration of the Renaissance conviction that the business of literature is to instruct and delight.

As one would expect in any large community the boys come in all temperaments and in all shapes and sizes:

> The healers and the brilliant talkers,
> The eccentrics and the silent walkers,
> The dumpy and the tall.

What they have in common is intelligence and academic potential which, of course, is what the entrance examination is designed to identify. Intelligence, however, is no guarantee of effort and although nearly all of them are highly motivated some, inevitably, are idle and imagine that native wit alone will see them through. The school does its best to disabuse them. There are others, not many but they exist, whose considerable intelligence has made them unfamiliar with difficulty and consequently they have not developed the ability to 'tough it out' when things do become difficult. But in the vast majority intelligence combines with hard work to realise potential to its fullest extent, with the restult that in the school as a whole there is an atmosphere of great intellectual efficiency. What most Edwardians lack, however, is flamboyance, though there have been notable exceptions. For instance, during the war Kenneth Tynan in one of his more exuberant moments electrified the diners in the British Restaurant in nearby Selly Oak by leaping on to a table and delivering an impassioned discourse on the merits of free love.

If some may miss at King Edward's what appears as intellectual fizz in comparable metropolitan schools (e.g. St Paul's School or Dulwich College) that does not mean that intellectual vitality is any less vigorous; it merely means that the *mores* of Birmingham are not quite those of London and that a greater stolidity is a feature of the local style. The Edwardian is not one to take chances and has always kept his cards close to his chest. He guards carefully against giving too much away. This reserve is not so much evident in personal relations as in the classroom where intellectual competition is strong and a prudent caution, which should not be mistaken for passivity, reigns. Some people, including some of the girls next door, have found him inclined to arrogance and probably there is some truth in this, though no more than would be true of boys in comparable schools. A partial explanation may be that the school's record of success since the war and the increasing media attention which this success has received and the general attitude to the school in Birmingham combine to make it difficult for a boy who gains entry not to believe that he is one of the chosen. The 'pursuit of excellence' is a good thing but to be always hearing about it can have unfortunate side effects. There is no doubt, however, that these talented, lively boys are a great pleasure to teach and to know, and one of the most heartening features about them is that when one meets them ten, twenty, thirty years after they have left school what civilised and stimulating men they are. It would be nice to think that the school has something to do with this.

Members of the Joint Orchestra were brought into service by the Personal Service Group to provide entertainment in an inner city school. Ruth Wilkinson plays the horn and Kevin Greenbank the trumpet.

It would not be much of an exaggeration to say that at any one time the two most important people in the school are the Head Porter and the Chief Master's secretary. For most of the period from 1950 to 1990 only two men have ruled in the porters' lodge, Bert Allard and Jack Bailey. Allard was an old Coldstreamer whom Canon Lunt caused to be appointed at the start of his Chief Mastership. He was known to the boys as 'Such' because when he arrived the school captain of the day informed the school that 'the new head porter is called Allard and will be known as such'. He was described by the head groundsman, Jack Holden, the former British marathon runner, as 'an amiable rogue'. But he was an honest rogue, a marvellous fixer, almost invariably cheerful, a big and impressive-looking man, always brisk and bustling in movement and full of helpful ideas. One step lower in the portering hierarchy was Henry Craddock, last encountered earlier in this chapter trapped inside a vaulting-box. He had a splendidly large square jaw apparently made out of granite and a wooden leg that really lived up to its name. It swung and creaked its way indomitably round the building as Craddock moved about his daily tasks. He had a sharp intelligence and the moment when his rocky face slowly cracked into a slight grin of scornful scepticism was something to treasure.

Allard's successor, Jack Bailey, a former RSM in the Northumberland Fusiliers, resembled him in knowing absolutely everything that happened in the school and, if he had decided that you were all right, being able to fix anything for you. As a personality, however, he was quite different, totally without 'flannel' (of which Allard had quite a share), apparently grim but in fact very shrewd and amusing, full of sardonic observation ('The school's all right, it's just the bloody masters') and, if you passed his character test, a marvellous source of friendly and helpful support. He literally worked himself to death for the school rather than pull out when his health was already far from good.

Hugh Wright was appointed
Chief Master in 1991.

In 1950 the Chief Master's secretary, Freda Minshull, had already been twenty years in the job. She had worked for England, Morris and Howarth and was to carry on well into the Lunt era. There was, in consequence, practically nothing about the workings of the school that she did not know. Lunt's greeting when she brought some tea into a heads of departments meeting – 'Dear Miss Minshull, what a Florence Nightingale you are!' – could have related equally truly to a hundred and one other things that she did. And so too of Joyce Gibbs who retired in 1988 after seventeen years in the job under Lunt, Fisher and Rogers. In both of these ladies knowledge of the school, tact, patience and unfailing good humour appeared to be limitless.

In 1952 Hutton wrote that the school 'is doing . . . not less than it did even in its greatest days'. He does not say when its greatest days were but it is fairly clear that he had in mind some period, not too closely specified, in the nineteenth century. Yet one might plausibly argue that in 1952 'its greatest days' were still to come. Our attempts to pinpoint a supposed 'golden age' will depend upon what we believe to constitute it. Was it one which produced the most eminent or brilliant men in public life? the most eminent scholars? the most consistently good examination results? the most creative changes? the most Common Room 'characters'? the most whizzing Chief Master(s)? If, however, we accept Vardy's admirable dictum that 'schools exist mainly for the average boy' then how the average boy fares is clearly a prime factor in our choice of a 'golden age'. Such a criterion would certainly suggest placing the golden age in the twentieth century rather than in the nineteenth and we must add another criterion, the range of activities pursued without any diminution of academic excellence. This edges us inescapably towards the second half of the twentieth century. If it seems that what is being proposed is a crudely quantitative assessment one can only say that King Edward's School has kept up with the widening conception of education that the last hundred years have brought, and that in most of these new activities and fields of study it has achieved something of the distinction that Prince Lee brought to its classical studies. The post-war period has seen the school produce an England rugger international, an England tourist and Barbarian, a test cricketer, two other county cricketers and several junior cricketers who have reached international teams at their respective age-levels as have several basketball players, a schoolboy swimming international and a schoolboy international javelin thrower. Excellence is spread wider. But whether the Edwardian of the period 1950–90 grows into a more civilised man, or is better fitted to cope usefully with the world in which he has to live than his predecessor a hundred years before, is a question that in Sir Thomas Browne's phrase 'might admit a wide solution'.

It does not do to be too solemn about schools, particularly in an age which is as obsessively divided about education as that of 'our pious founder and benefactor' was about religion. If King Edward's School were to disappear tomorrow not only would the world still go round but Birmingham, although impoverished by the loss, would continue much as before. But that having been said, it must be said also that the school's contribution to the life and culture of the nation and the city, especially during the last 150 years, has been impressive. How impressive the Selected List of Old Edwardians will show. At

PLATE 7

Left: Boys leaving school down the Main Drive, *c.* 1950. This photograph has particular value in showing a rear view of Henry Craddock returning from a mission to the Foundation Office, wooden leg in purposeful action.

Below: The building in the left centre of the picture was the former Liberal Club which became, for several years, the home of King Edward's High School for Girls while their own school was being built on the site of the Hen and Chickens in New Street.

PLATE 8   A view of the south front of the present building across the South Field, site of the former temporary buildings.

the time of writing King Edward's is going great guns; its academic successes are unrivalled, it is expanding the range of its activities as well as its numbers, it has increased its plant and its Common Room has a high proportion of very able young teachers. It fulfils the educational *desiderata* of our age with enormous success. But it faces a more difficult task and a more serious responsibility. In the present age of technology and economics it is more than ever important to be faithful to the values that have nourished 'good learning' at all times, a belief in the worth of what is immaterial and unquantifiable, not just as a necessary complement to the prevailing code of 'getting and spending' but as essential to fully human living. It is too early yet to see how the school will measure up to this challenge but one thing is certain, that failure to do so will be to betray the spirit that animated the lives of so many of its most distinguished sons.

Mourning the passing of the Master's Quiet Room (known as the Geriatric Ward) on the last day of its use before extensive alterations abolished it in 1989. Heads from left to right: Brian Tomlinson, Martin Stead, Tim Jayne, John Clark, David Hill, Maurice Workman, Tony Trott, Philip Lambie, John Hatton, Derek Everest, Graham Underhill and Mike Hopley.

King Edward's School Song

Written by Alfred Hayes OE (1857–1936). Music by A. Somervell

Where the iron heart of England throbs beneath its sombre robe,
Stands a school whose sons have made her great and famous round the globe,
These have plucked the bays of battle, those have won the scholar's crown;
Old Edwardians, young Edwardians, forward for the school's renown.

Chorus
Forward where the knocks are hardest, some to failure, some to fame;
Never mind the cheers or hooting, keep your head and play the game.

Here's no place for fop or idler; they who made our city great
Feared no hardship, shirked no labour, smiled at death and conquered fate;
They who gave our school its laurels laid on us a sacred trust;
Forward therefore, live your hardest, die of service, not of rust.

Forward where the scrimmage thickens; never stop to rub your shin;
Cowards count the kicks and ha'pence, only care to save their skin.
Oftentimes defeat is splendid, victory may still be shame;
Luck is good, the prize is pleasant, but the glory's in the game.

Here no classic grove secludes us, here abides no cloistered calm;
Not the titled nor the stranger, wrestles here to gain the palm;
Round our smoke-encrusted precincts labour's turbid river runs;
Builders of this burly city temper here their strenuous sons.

The last stanza was dropped when the school moved from New Street to Edgbaston as being
no longer strictly true. This was a pity as it is the only stanza not to deal in standard school-song
clichés.

Quatercentenary Song

Written by Roger Dunt, composed by Willis Grant

Quadringentos iam per annos
  schola haec nutrivit
haud ingratos nos alumnos
  nosque stabilivit.
Nunc feramus, nunc canamus
  regi nostro grates.
Edwardum Edwardum regem celebramus.

Rex fundavit, instauravit
  scholam hanc dilectam;
urbs amavit, conservavit
  tutam ac protectam.
Nunc feramus, nunc canamus
  urbi nostrae grates.
Edwardum Edwardum regem celebramus.

Procedamus, gaudeamus
  iuvenili mente;
studeamus, floreamus
  in florenti gente.
Nunc feramus, nunc canamus
  almae matri grates.
Edwardum Edwardum regem celebramus.

Iam reginae, Glorianae
  alteri, venustae,
disciplinae ac doctrinae
  memori vetustae,
nunc feramus, nunc canamus
  haud ingrati grates
Elissam Elissam reginam celebramus.

The last stanza was added for the visit of Queen Elizabeth II on 3 November 1955.

The Founder's Prayer

We give Thee most humble and hearty thanks, O most merciful Father, for our pious founder, King Edward the Sixth, and for all our governors and benefactors by whose benefit this whole School is brought up to godliness and good learning; and we beseech Thee to give us grace to use these Thy blessings to the glory of Thy holy Name, that we may answer the good intent of our religious founder, and become profitable members of the Church and commonwealth, and at last be partakers of Thy heavenly kingdom; through our Lord and Saviour, Jesus Christ.

A form of this prayer, giving thanks for William of Wykeham, had long been in use at Winchester when Thomas Arnold was at the school as a boy. When he later became Headmaster of Rugby School he adapted it for use there. When his protégé, James Prince Lee, came to Birmingham in 1838 as Chief Master of King Edward's School he introduced it, suitably adapted again, for use here.

Selected List of Old Edwardians

(The date after each man's name is, as nearly as can be ascertained, the date when he left school)

RICHARD COLMORE (*c.* 1565) Fellow of Brasenose College, Oxford; Chancellor of Durham; Commissioner to treat with the Scots about border disputes (1595).

RICHARD BILLINGSLEY (*c.* 1585) Probably an OE Fellow of Brasenose College, Oxford; Chief Master of KES (1599–?1639); Demoted to Usher (?1640).

RICHARD SHILTON (*c.* 1595–1600) Treasurer of the Inner Temple; Solicitor-General (1625–34); MP for Bridgnorth; governor of KES.

PAUL FOLEY (*c.* 1660–5) Speaker of the House of Commons (1695).

JOHN HOUGH (*c.* 1668) President of Magdalen College, Oxford, elected in defiance of James II (1686); Bishop of Oxford (1690); translated to Lichfield (1699) and thence to Worcester (1717); declined the Primacy (1715).

RICHARD SMALBROKE (*c.* 1688) Bishop of St David's (1724), translated to Lichfield (1731).

JOHN TURTON (1752) FRS (1763); FRCP (1767); Physician-in-Ordinary to the Queen (1782).

RICHARD VYSE (*c.* 1762) Commander of the 1st Dragoon Guards in Flanders (1784); Major-General (1794); General (1812); Controller to the Duke of Cumberland.

CHRISTOPHER PEGGE (*c.* 1782) FRS (1795); Regius Professor of Physics at Oxford.

RANN KENNEDY (*c.* 1790) A fine classical scholar and father of four other fine classical scholars; Usher's assistant at KES (1799–1804); Chief Master's assistant (1804–8); Usher (1808–36); Incumbent of St Paul's, Hockley (1796–1851).

HENRY CARY (*c.* 1790) Translator of Dante's *La Divina Comedia* (1805–14); Aristophanes' *The Birds* (1824); Pindar (1832). Published at the age of fifteen and while at KES an ode to Lord Heathfield, defender of Gibraltar, where Cary was born.

DAVID COX (*c.* 1795) Artist; alleged to have attended the grammar school in Birmingham.

JOHN RADFORD (*c.* 1801) Rector of Lincoln College, Oxford (1834).

JOSEPH HODGSON (*c.* 1804) FRS. One of the founders of the Birmingham Eye Infirmary (1824); President of the Royal College of Surgeons (1864).

EDWARD GRAINGER (*c.* 1815) At the age of twenty-two founded an anatomy school in London. Born the same year as Franz Schubert and two years after John Keats, his life like theirs was short. He died at the age of twenty-seven.

BENJAMIN KENNEDY (1819) Son of Rann Kennedy he was, at the age of fifteen, removed to Shrewsbury School where he later became headmaster and author of the indispensable and dreaded *Latin Primer*. Professor of Greek at Cambridge (1867).

EDWIN GUEST (1819) Lawyer, antiquarian, philologist (*A History of English Rhythm*), farmer; elected to the Mastership of Gonville and Caius College, Cambridge, by his own deciding vote.

WILLIAM SANDS COX (*c.* 1819) One of the founders of the Queen's Hospital, Birmingham (1841); founded medical scholarships at KES.

WILLIAM MARTIN (1826) Kt; first Chief Justice of New Zealand; advocate of native rights.

W. LINWOOD (1835) Winner of Herford, Ireland and Craven Prizes at Oxford all in the same year; editor of *Aeschylus*.

FRANCIS GALTON (*c.* 1840) Explorer in the Sudan and S. W. Africa, anthropologist and meteorologist; he established the existence of anticyclones and explained them and laid the foundations for the science of eugenics.

CHARLES EVANS (1843) Chief Master of KES (1862–72).

J. S. PURTON (1843) Master of St Catherine's College, Cambridge.

BROOKE FOSS WESTCOTT (1844) Regius Professor of Divinity at Cambridge; Bishop of Durham (1890).

JOSEPH BARBER LIGHTFOOT (1847) Hulsean Professor of Divinity (1855); Lady Margaret Professor of Divinity (1875); Bishop of Durham (1879). A socialist tendency in his speeches prevented his translation to London.

JOHN CONOLLY (1847) Lieut.-Col.; a boarder in Prince Lee's house; winner of the VC in the Crimea; decorated a month after the Battle of the Alma.

E. J. PURBRICK (1847) Provincial of the Society of Jesus in England and then in USA.

EDWARD WHITE BENSON (1848) Headmaster of Wellington College (1859); Bishop of Truro (1877); Archbishop of Canterbury (1883).

R. W. DIXON (1852) Canon of Carlisle and author of *A History of the Church of England from the Abolition of the Roman Jurisdiction*; minor poet; friend of Gerard Manley Hopkins and earliest admirer of his poetry.

EDWARD BURNE JONES (1852) Kt; Artist and friend of Dixon.

EDWIN HATCH (1853) Professor of Classics at Toronto University; Vice-Principal of St Mary's Hall, Oxford; Reader in Ecclesiastical History and Bampton Lecturer; friend of Burne Jones and Dixon.

CORNELL PRICE (1854) First headmaster of United Services College, Westward Ho! The model for 'Bates' in Kipling's *Stalky & Co.* Friend of Dixon and Burne Jones.

ALEXANDER MACKENZIE (1859) Kt; Chief Commissioner, Central Province of India; Chief Commissioner, Burma (1895); Lieu.-Governor of Bengal.

JAMES SMITH (*c.* 1864–65) Kt; last Mayor and first Lord Mayor of Birmingham (1895–6).

JOHN CHURTON COLLINS (1867) Literary critic; exposer of the superficial scholarship of Sir Edmund Gosse; a tireless and belligerent advocate of the cause of English studies at Oxford; did not get the chair when it was finally founded; Professor of English at Birmingham University.

R. G. KEKEWICH (1867) CB; Maj.-General; Defender of Kimberly; died of wounds, 5 Nov. 1914.

NATHAN BODINGTON (1867) Kt; Litt. D; Appointed head of Yorkshire College of

Science – guided it through several stages to become Leeds University (1904).

WILLIAM BOWATER (*c.* 1871–72) Kt; Lord Mayor of Birmingham five times between 1909 and 1915.

W. NAPIER SHAW (1872) Kt; FRS (1891); Director of the Meteorological Office (1915); President of the International Meteorological Society (1907–23).

A. W. DALE (1874) Kt; Principal of University College, Liverpool (1899), Vice-Chancellor when university status was granted (1903).

J. F. BETHUNE-BAKER (1881) Lady Margaret Professor of Theology at Cambridge; Dean of Pembroke College; FBA.

W. P. WYNNE (1882) Professor of Chemistry, Sheffield University (1904–31).

F. W. THOMAS (1885) CIE; FBA; D. Litt.; Librarian to the India Office; Boden Professor of Sanscrit at Oxford; one of the school's very finest scholars.

A. E. W. HAZEL (1887) Kt; Principal of Jesus College, Oxford. Classic and lawyer. Recorder of Burton-on-Trent (1912–38); MP for West Bromwich (1906–10).

WALTER MYERS (1888) Died at the age of twenty-nine in Brazil, leading an expedition from the Liverpool School of Tropical Medicine investigating the cause of yellow fever.

E. W. BARNES (1893) A very eminent mathematician. Fellow and Tutor of Trinity College, Cambridge; FRS; Master of the Temple (1908–15); Canon of Westminster (1918); Bishop of Birmingham (1924); governor of KES.

C. F. ANDREWS (1890) A considerable scholar in classics and theology and a good sportsman; vice-president of Westcott House, Cambridge. But his main work was in India where he went in 1909 with the Cambridge Mission to Delhi. He was much influenced by Tagore and Gandhi. A contemporary Indian politician has said that 'he did more for the people of India than all the viceroys'. Nicknamed 'the friend of India'.

HOLLAND HOBBISS (1896) Architect. He designed the present school buildings and the Union building of Birmingham University.

B. OUGHTRED (1898) England rugger international (1901–3); captain (1903).

RICHARD HOPKINS (1899) Kt; Secretary to the Treasury and Head of the Civil Service (1943–5).

F. H. VINEY (1901) School governor and benefactor.

A. W. IBBOTSON (1905) Kt; Indian Civil Service.

E. W. ASSINDER (1905) England rugger international (1908–9).

P. J. DANIELL (1907) Professor of Mathematics, University of Sheffield.

H. C. HARRISON (1907) England rugger international (1909 and 1914).

T. W. HUTTON (1907) Editor of the *Birmingham Post*; historian of the school and governor.

F. P. WILSON (1908) Merton Professor of English Literature in the University of Oxford (1947–57).

DONALD FINNEMORE (1908) High Court Judge in the Queen's Bench and school governor.

SIDNEY BARNES (1908) Kt; Secretary to the Admiralty.

H. V. MORTON (1909) Author of books largely about places.

STANLEY ASTBURY (1909) MC; Principal of Chester Training College; Principal of Army Padres' Training Centre.

T. C. KEMP (1909) Drama critic and author.

WILLIAM SLIM (1910) Viscount: KG; GCB; DSO; MC; Field-Marshal; Victor of Burma; Governor-General of Australia.

J. R. R. TOLKIEN (1911) CBE; Professor of English Language, University of Leeds (1924); Professor of Anglo-Saxon at Oxford (1925); Merton Professor of English Language and Literature at Oxford (1945); fantasy novelist of great fame.

ROBERT SAUNDBY (1914) Kt; MC; DFC; Air-Marshal.

MICHAEL TERRY (1915) Rode a motor-bike (picked up for a song) across Australia from north to south (or perhaps from south to north). Stayed to become an authority on the aborigines and their culture.

C. E. N. GUEST (1916) Kt; KBE; CB; Air-Marshal.

WILLIAM GILPIN (1920) Bishop of Kingston-upon-Thames (1952); Bishop Gilpin School in Wimbledon named after him; a railway buff.

F. H. SANDBACH (1922) Professor of Classics at Cambridge.

RAYMOND HUNTLEY (1922) Actor on stage, in films and television.

ROY PASCAL (1923) Professor of German, Birmingham University. Member of the CP but left it in the early 1950s before the Hungarian uprising.

GODFREY WINN (1924) Journalist and broadcaster· South of England Junior Lawn Tennis Champion at the age of thirteen.

RICHARD WATTIS (1926) Actor on stage, in films and television.

DONALD DUDLEY (1928) Professor of Latin at Birmingham University; governor of KES.

ROBERT HARVEY (1928) OBE; governor of KES (1968–).

C. H. O'D ALEXANDER (1928) The strongest British chess player of the inter-war period; worked among the backroom boffins at Bletchley Park during the war; chess columnist.

A. N. MAY (1929) Atomic scientist involved in passing information to Moscow. Professor of Physics, University of Ghana.

F. J. ('Eric') Williams (1929) Classics master at KES (1937–72); head of department (1963–72); school chaplain (1952–72).

J. ENOCH POWELL (1930) PC; MBE; Professor of Greek at Sydney University (1937–9); Brigadier; MP for Wolverhampton West (1950–74); Financial Secretary to the Treasury (1957–8); Minister of Health (1960–3); MP for South Down (1974–87).

ERIC HILL (1930) Prebendary Emeritus and Honorary Librarian of Lichfield Cathedral; responsible for the retranslation of St Chad's Bible.

ARNOLD GOUREVITCH (1931) MC; a Commando doctor, a surgeon at the Queen Elizabeth Hospital, Birmingham; went post-haste to serve in Israel during the Six Days War. A keen golfer.

R. A. S. MARTINEAU (1932) Bishop of Huntingdon (1966); Bishop of Blackburn (1972–81).

GEORGE PAINTER (1932) Biographer of Marcel Proust and André Gide.

DENIS HILLS (1932) At the end of the Second World War his Scarlet Pimpernel activities preserved many Poles from certain execution if returned to their homeland; author of an authoritative book on Turkey. Lecturer at Makerere University, Uganda; condemned to death by Idi Amin; released on the personal intervention of the Prime Minister, James Callaghan.

ROWLAND RYDER (1933) Biographer and cricket writer.

J. E. GENDERS (1933) Chief Personnel Executive for Guardian Royal Exchange Assurance Ltd; Vice-President, Institute of Personnel Managers (1972–4); chairman of the Central Committee of Help the Aged and of Brackenbridge House.

JOHN EAYRS (1933) Professor of Anatomy at the Queen Elizabeth Hospital, Birmingham.

PETER MASON (1933) High Master of Manchester Grammar School (1962–78).

ROBERT CASE (1934) FRCP; Emeritus Professor of Social Medicine, London. His last article (1990), published in the journal of the Sands Cox Soc. was intriguingly entitled 'Bleeding Bladders, Brum and Brummies'.

ROBERT GARRATT (1935) DFC; governor of KES and Chairman of the Governors' Independent Schools Committe (1965–).

M. H. F. WILKINS (1935) Sharer in the Nobel Prize for Medicine and Physiology for work on the structure of DNA.

DENIS SMALLWOOD (1936) Kt; DSO; DFC; Air Chief Marshal; C-in-C RAF Strike Command (1974); C-in-C RAF in the UK (1975).

BEN DAVIS (1937) Home office Consultant on Forensic Medicine.

M. D. K. DAUNCEY (1937) Brigadier; Military Attaché in Madrid.

ARTHUR DAVIES (1938) High Court Judge (1972).

H. L. JAMES (1938) Director-General of the National Association of Pension Funds; Press Secretary to Margaret Thatcher (1979).

R. M. GENDERS (1938) Member of the Community of the Resurrection; Bishop of Bermuda (1977–82).

P. W. EDWARDS (1939) King Alfred Professor of English Literature, University of Liverpool.

TOM FREEMAN (1939) Cambridge Cricket Blue.

R. W. EVANS (1939) Managing Director and Chief Executive of the Rank Organisation.

J. E. H. COLLINS (1939) Chairman of the Guardian Royal Exchange Assurance Ltd.

P. G. Bevan (1940) Professor of Surgery, University of Birmingham.

F. O. Hooley (1940) MP for the Heeley Division of Sheffield.

B. D. Bush (1941) High Court Judge.

A. E. Marsland (1941) Professor of Dentistry and Vice-Chancellor of Birmingham University.

B. H. McGowan (1942) Headmaster of Market Raisen GS, of Solihull School and of Haberdashers Aske's School at Elstree. Chairman of the Headmasters' Conference (1985).

P. Hollingworth (1942) Lord Mayor of Birmingham (1982).

Eric Handley (1943) FBA; Regius Professor of Greek at Cambridge.

E. W. Parkes (1943) Kt; Vice-Chancellor of Leeds University; Chairman of the University Grants Committee.

Colin Figures (1944) Kt; Deputy Secretary to the Cabinet Office.

Maurice Shock (1944) Vice-Chancellor of Leicester University; Chairman of the Committee of Vice-Chancellors; Rector of Lincoln College, Oxford.

J. R. Vane (1944) Kt; Nobel Prize Winner; Director of Group Research and Development, the Wellcome Research Labs.

Kenneth Tynan (1945) Dedicated to work and cricket at school and to being an *enfant terrible* at Oxford he emerged as the brilliant drama critic of the *Observer* newspaper; propagandist for the drama of Bertold Brecht when that drama was hardly ever seen on the English stage; Literary Adviser to the National Theatre.

P. Laister (1946) Chairman and Chief Executive, Thorn EMI.

R. Heron (1946) Director of the Duke of Edinburgh Award Scheme.

J. H. Hollingworth (1946) MP for All Saints, Birmingham (1959–64). He had a majority of 20 – a damned close-run thing.

Michael Apps (1947) SSF; Guardian of Hillfield Priory, Dorchester (1978–89).

Peter Jackson (1947) England rugger international.

John Hamlin (1949) Although he left KES after only two years he made amends by returning to teach at the school (1960–6); headmaster of Reigate Grammar School.

Peter Walters (1949) Kt; Chairman of British Petroleum.

C. F. B. Laughland (1950) Defence counsel in the trial of Clive Ponting; High Court Judge.

Gavin Lyall (1951) Novelist.

Graham Tayar (1951) Executive Producer, BBC Schools Radio; Head of Audio/Radio for the SAAG Consortium; Media/Education Consultant.

R. A. Tomlinson (1951) Professor of Archaeology, Birmingham University.

Frederick Oxley (1951) FRCO; organist and Master of the Choristers, St Edmundsbury Cathedral (1958–84); conductor of the St Edmundsbury Bach Choir and Orchestra; recitalist.

J. F. Wainwright (1951) Warden of Glen Almond Academy, Perth; Cambridge rugger blue (1956).

A. G. B. Haselhurst (1951) Left at the end of his third year after a winsome performance as Madame Pons in Jules Romains' play, *Dr Knock*; MP for Saffron Walden, PS to the Sec. of State for Education and Science (1979–81).

Michael McClean (1951) Canon Residentiary and Chancellor of Norwich Cathedral.

John Ling (1952) Foreign Office (1959–78); MEP for East Warwickshire (1979–89).

Barry Leek (1953) Professor of Vetinary Science at Bristol and Dublin Universities.

Peter Steward (1953) FRSE; Professor of Histo-chemistry, Dundee University; Visiting Professor, Pavia University since 1980.

Colin Gilbraith (1953) Treasurer and Tutor, Pembroke College, Cambridge.

Derek Benson (1953) Returned to KES in 1962 to teach chemistry and as master in charge of cricket, a job which he did with great success for twenty-one years.

O. S. ('Ossie') Wheatley (1953) Cambridge cricket blue; capped for Warwickshire CCC and Glamorgan CCC; captain of Glamorgan and subsequently President; Chairman of the Cricket Committee of the TCCB.

Brian Cleaver (1953) Lecturer in Chemistry at the University of Southampton.

Arthur Stockwin (1954) Nissan Professor of Modern Japanese Studies, Oxford.

John Vernon (1954) Lecturer in Chemistry at the University of York.

Michael Hodgetts (1954) Member of the Catholic International Commission on English in the Liturgy.

Brian Kington (1954) A long career with IBM, in their development laboratories and in their education and training operation and external relations with Education and Science; a member of the Society of Industrial Liaison Officers; consultant in educational and business partnerships.

David Buttress (1954) Head of History and subsequently Deputy Chief Master at KES, the first King Edward's ever in such honour named.

David Gallon (1954) Deputy Regional Director, London Area, the Open University.

David Lomax (1954) After some time in the FO transferred to the National Westminster Bank where he is a senior economics adviser.

John Evans (1955) Professor of Geriatric Medicine, Oxford (1985).

David Rudkin (1955) Dramatist and translator.

Anthony Hodgetts (1955) Member of the Congregation of the Redeemer; lecturer at Beda College, Rome.

David Witherow (1955) Deputy Director, BBC World Service.

ALAN SMITH (1955) Captain of Oxford University CC and Warwickshire CCC; MCC tourist in Australia (1961–2) where he played in four Tests; Sec. of Warwickshire CCC and Chief Executive of the TCCB.

PETER SQUIRE (1955) Headmaster, Bedford Modern School.

KONRAD SCHIEMANN (1955) High Court Judge.

BARRY GANE (1955) OBE; Counsellor FO.

JOHN DREW (1955) Head of the London Office of the European Commission.

GAVIN MILLAR (1956) For many years film correspondent of the *Listener*; broadcaster and film director; author of books on film.

ROGER WILSON (1956) Headmaster of HM Duke of Kent School, Ewhurst; captain of school rugger in 1956 when KES won the Public Schools Sevens.

CHRISTOPHER LONG (1956) CMG; HM Ambassador in Berne.

JOHN GOODE (1956) Professor of English Literature, Keele University.

RICHARD DUNCAN-JONES (1956) Fellow and Director of Studies in Classics at Gonville and Caius College, Cambridge.

NATHAN JOSEPH (1957) Entrepreneur; he has been successful on both sides of the Atlantic in music publishing and is now a theatrical producer and agent; member of the Council of the Theatrical Managers' Assoc. and of the Theatre Advisory Council.

PETER VAUGON (1957) Deputy Secretary-General, Cambridge University.

CHRISTOPHER GANE (1957) Computer Systems Development Consultant in USA; author of several authoritative books on computer systems.

ROBERT SWEENEY (1957) Vicar of St Thomas with St Frideswide, Oxford; chaplain, Magdalen College (1982).

MARTIN SWALES (1958) Professor of German, University College, London.

NICHOLAS McCARTY (1958) Television dramatist.

R. Y. CARTWRIGHT (1958) Professor of Microbiology, University of Reading.

A. COWIE (1958) Military Attaché, Budapest.

JOHN PEEL (1959) Professor of Sociology, Liverpool University.

JOHN JORDAN (1959) FRCO; Master of Music, Chelmsford Cathedral (1965–81); President of the IAO (1975–7); Director of Music Studies, Yamaha Music School, Kuching, Sarawak (1988–91).

BERNARD RICHARDS (1959) Fellow of Brasenose College, Oxford, and Director of Studies in English.

ROBERT SMALLWOOD (1959) Director of Courses at the Shakespeare Centre, Stratford-upon-Avon.

THOMAS SHIPPEY (1960) Professor of English Language and Medieval Literature at the University of Leeds.

DAVID MUNROW (1960) Musician extraordinary; a dynamic pioneer in the performance and dissemination of medieval music; a brilliant deviser of radio programmes about music; a veritable *rara avis*.

DAVID WINKLEY (1960) A career devoted to interests forgotten by most OEs – primary education; headmaster of Grove Junior School, Handsworth, from 1975, he has at the same time been Fellow of Nuffield College, Oxford (1983–5), a member of the Council for the Accreditation of Teacher Education (1986–90), a founder and director of the National Primary Centre (1988) and written a book on the Schools Inspectorate. Another rare bird.

MICHAEL REEVE (1960) Won both the Craven and Ireland Prizes in his first year at Oxford; Professor of Latin at Cambridge.

DAVID FREMLIN (1960) Won the Smith Prize, the highest award for mathematics at Cambridge; Reader in Mathematics at the University of Essex.

JOHN FERNS (1960) When a sixth-former he ran in the school cross-country race wearing L-plates, not a popular move with the PE Dept. Later became Professor of English, MacMasters University, Canada. He has published several collections of poetry.

JOHN FIELD (1960) For many years head of English and of Drama and Director of Studies at Westminster School; the historian of that school.

BILL ODDIE (1960) Humourist, entertainer, scriptwriter, television performer, bird-watcher. Winner of the Silver Rose Award at the Montreux Festival.

RICHARD GREENHILL (1961) Consultant neurologist, Oxford Hospitals.

ALISTAIR PAPPS (1961) Governor of Durham and Frankland Prisons; Manager of Prisons for the North-East Area.

JOHN GOLDINGAY (1961) Principal of St John's College, Nottingham.

MALCOLM LEE (1961) QC; Recorder of the Crown Court.

B. B. D. MERRY (1961) Professor of Italian, Witwatersrand University, S. Africa.

GEOFFREY SKELSEY (1962) Head of the Vice-Chancellor's Office, Cambridge University.

R. W. BRAY (1962) Professor of Music, University of Lancaster.

PATTERSON FERNS (1962) Founder President of Primedia Entertainments Inc., Canada.

JOHN DEATHRIDGE (1963) Musician; Wagner buff; Fellow of King's College, Cambridge.

JOHN BURGESS (1964) Literary Manager, the National Theatre, the post first held by Kenneth Tynan.

JOHN CROXALL (1964) Principal Scientific Officer and section head in the British Antarctic Survey; Scientific Medallist of the Zool. Soc. of London (1984).

ANTHONY HEY (1964) Reader in Theoretical Physics, Southampton University (1983–6), Professor of Computation, Electronics & Computer Science (1986–).

PAUL GRIFFITHS (1965) Music critic of *The Times*; novelist and librettist.

PETER HANFORD (1965) Director of Research, Law Reform Commission, W. Australia.

HARRY HINE (1966) Professor of Humanities, St Andrew's University.

F. J. GOULDING (1966) Director of Music and permanent conductor, D'Oyly Carte Opera Company School.

JONATHAN LEE (1966) Headmaster, Trent College.

CHRISTOPHER FERNS (1967) Associate Professor of English, Mount St Vincent University, Canada.

DAVID HILL (1967) Director of Communications, Labour Party HQ.

R. J. ARCULUS (1967) Professor of Geology, University of New England, Australia.

DAVID DUTTON (1968) Lecturer in History, University of Liverpool.

GEOFFREY GRIMMETT (1968) British Olympic Fencing Team; lecturer in mathematics, Bristol University.

ANDREW FREEMAN (1970) Swam for Gt. Britain Juniors against Holland and Germany (1969); broke the Gt. Britain Junior hundred yards swimming record (1969).

KEVIN LEE (1970) Actor and playwright. Winner of the Writers Guild Award (1991).

CHRISTOPHER LIGHTFOOT (1973) Deputy Director of the British School at Ankara.

STEPHEN BADSEY (1973) Imperial War Museum; consultant on military matters for several television productions; lecturer at RMC Sandhurst.

TONY MILES (1973) World Junior Chess Champion; first British grandmaster.

CHARLES SPICER (1973) Actor.

DAVID FOSTER (1974) OSB Downside.

SCOTT NEWTON (1974) Lecturer in Modern Economic History, Cardiff University.

JAMES LAWLEY (1974) Formerly co-principal of the Centro Inglese, Avila; since 1988 lecturer in English, Madrid University.

DAVID WILLETTS (1974) Graduated from castigating the floppy overcoats and unruly tresses of his seniors when in C1.VA to the Directorship of the Conservative Centre for Policy Studies; M.P. for Havant (1992).

PAUL SMITH (1974) British Council; after several uncomfortable years spreading the British way of life in West Africa he claims the sobriquet 'Smith of the Coast'. He was rewarded with several years lotus-eating in London, vetting plays for British Council export support.

IAN HARVEY (1974) Lecturer in Social Medicine at Cardiff University.

JOHN CLAUGHTON (1975) Oxford cricket blue who then played for Warwickshire CCC; Classics master and master in charge of cricket, Eton College.

JONATHAN GIBBS (1975) Head of editing and post-production sound at the BBC Television Centre.

MICHAEL JOHN (1975) Historian, Fellow of Magdalen College, Oxford.

ANDREW HUDSON (1976) PS to the Minister of State, Treasury.

IAN METCALFE (1977) Cambridge rugger blue; toured New Zealand with an England XV, and played for the Barbarians.

BRIAN CUMMINGS (1978) Research Fellow, Trinity College, Cambridge; lecturer in English at the University of Sussex.

MARK STEYN (1978) Journalist, broadcaster, authority on musicals.

NEIL HARVEY (1978) Artist.

JONATHAN COE (1979) Novelist and novel reviewer for the *Guardian* newspaper.

FREDERICK DUNSTAN (1979) Novelist and artist.

JAMES MILES (1979) BBC journalist. Won the Sony Radio Journalist of the Year Award for his coverage of events in China in 1989.

CHRISTOPHER GRIMLEY (1985) Basketball Player of the Year in the State of California (1985–6).

Appendix 1:

Feuds within the Governing Body leading up to the
Chancery Case of 1604

The Smalbroke and Colmore families, both 'founder members', as it were, of the Free Grammar School were also allied by marriage, Thomas Smalbroke having married Elizabeth Colmore in 1570. But marriage is no guarantee against family rivalry. Smalbroke was well known as a ruthless and covetous man of business as well as being an eager and formidable litigant, one, moreover, whose loyalties since he had become Steward of the Manor appeared to be uncertain. On the other side, William Colmore the elder, head of the Colmore clan, was domineering and, it seems, irascible and did not easily bear being crossed. One such crossing – and deeply resented it was – had occurred when Colmore's mother, remarried after the death of her Colmore husband, had tried to extract £400 from her son, William. Smalbroke had sided with his mother-in-law against his brother-in-law and had put his legal experience and finesse at her disposal. As a result it was Smalbroke rather than her son, William Colmore, who benefited from her will when she died. In this ulcer of family antagonisms Ambrose Colmore, brother of William and Constable of Birmingham, though not a governor of the school, seems to have allied himself with Smalbroke, his brother-in-law, rather than with William, his brother, and young William, his nephew. As both Smalbroke and William Colmore were governors of the school it is easy to see that school affairs could become a conduit through which their personal manoeuvrings and antipathies might flow. One can imagine governors' meetings as a kind of *champs clos* where family quarrels could be ritually fought out.

A prime example of this – the incident which gave rise to the Bill of Complaint of 1604 – had taken place twenty years earlier. It was briefly described by none other than the pedagogus of the school at the time, one William Woodwall, who, as will be seen, had no little interest in the incident. He wrote that there was:

> a robbery at Birmingham Church in Warwick of 2 rich velvet paul cloathes and a great summe of money which was the overplus of rents of the Grammar Schoole in that towne which ought to have been employed to the use of the Schoole master who was myself at that time. Done at Birmingham in Warwick 1583.

What happened was as follows. In the chancel of St Martin's Church was a chest, 'double and treble locked', in which the legal documents relating to the foundation of the school were kept. These documents had originally been in the keeping of Richard Smalbroke and when he died in 1575 they, along with the governors' seal and a substantial sum of money had been locked up in what may have been the parish chest. Because from 1578 the Rector of St Martin's, a certain Luke Smyth, was also a governor of the school it made sense to use what was probably the most secure safe place available rather than leave them in the School

House. The keys of the three locks were kept by three governors, one of them probably the rector of the church.

One night in 1583 the parish clerk, alerted perhaps by untoward noises, found on entering the church the contents of the chest strewn over the floor and most of the money gone. He hastened to awaken the town constable, Ambrose Colmore, who in his turn, went to arouse Thomas Smalbroke. Then, according to Colmore's story, he tried to call up his brother, William Colmore, but could not make anybody within the house hear him. So he returned to the church and, together with Thomas Smalbroke and the parish clerk and a neighbour of Smalbroke's who had tagged along, set about gathering up the scattered contents of the chest. The thieves had only been interested in the money and had even missed some of that which had been wrapped up in paper. The documents were put into boxes and taken into safe-keeping by Ambrose Colmore, who as constable was the proper person for such a responsibility. When this incident was used in the Chancery case against Smalbroke and Ambrose Colmore their opponents disputed that any attempt had been made to arouse William Colmore and implied that the defendants had deliberately managed things so as to possess the seal and the legal documents relating to the leases of foundation properties. As the town was expanding and property values were rising such possession could be of considerable value to the possessor. A further point at issue in the case was whether or not Smalbroke and Ambrose Colmore had subsequently relinquished possession of the seal and documents. The seventeen plaintiff governors claimed that they had not and also that Ambrose Colmore had kept the money that the thieves had overlooked. Somewhere among all this the charge was made that by their action Smalbroke and Ambrose Colmore brought about the 'utter ruin, spoil and overthrow of the Corporation and Free Grammar School'. The defendants disputed these accusations. No other governor sided with Smalbroke, which is a fair indication that he was not exactly loved but not proof that he was in the wrong. Certainly the Master-in-Chancery who heard the case did not think that he was and evidently accepted the defence that he and Ambrose Colmore were able to submit. The case was dismissed and Smalbroke had won again.

A question that may well have occurred to the thoughtful reader is why should there have been a gap of twenty years between the incident in St Martin's Church and the Bill of Complaint against Smalbroke and Colmore. What had finally pushed Smalbroke's fellow governors to risk taking him on on his own ground? Certainly the repercussions of the burglary had rumbled on during the intervening period, witness a governors' order of May 1596:

> Warne Mr. Smalbroke that hit ys further agreed that he shall bringe in to the greater part of the governors at the Schole house the xxiiij Day next after the feast of the annunciation of the Blessed Virgin next ensuing all the books Roles and writings concerninge the accompts of and the Rents of the said Schole lands ...
> Warne Mr. Ambrose Colmore to bring in to the said Governors the money he detyneth of Schole at the said xiiij days.

But Smalbroke was a formidable character with whom no one tangled lightly. It was said of him in court that 'he overreacheth most men with whom he has any dealing ... he is altogether a malicious and troublesome man and is so esteemed of the most part of his neighbours in the same town of Birmingham'. He was certainly aggressive and, what was worse, a natural winner. So although there seems to have been a strong current of feeling running against him it took some time for his enemies to nerve themselves for a legal confrontation. Even then their unanimity may have been fragile. It was suggested by Ambrose Colmore in the Chancery hearing that 'some of the parties named in the said Bill ... did not consent to the exhibiting thereof, as themselves have confessed, but the same is framed and devised ... by William Colmore the elder and William Colmore younger'.

Smalbroke's readiness to fight his enemies through the legal processes of which he was a master built up in them a powerful head of frustration and fury which increasingly sought satisfaction by other means, as for example, the composition and circulation of satirical verses at Smalbroke's expense in which his business dealings and methods were presented in a distinctly unfavourable (though probably fairly accurate) light. The author (or authors) of the lampoon in question remained anonymous but William Colmore and his supporters were the prime suspects and, indeed, Smalbroke later (1607) brought and won an action against them for libel as a result of which William Colmore was set in the pillory. And in his complaint on this issue to the Star Chamber Smalbroke included thirty-one names. His readiness to pursue them all at a high legal level seems to have decided his opponents to seek what was probably the most satisfying form of redress – violence.

One day in 1603 when Smalbroke, in the company of several neighbours, was working on his property Thomas Colmore and Thomas Holmes appeared in a rather menacing way, carrying long staves and, in Colmore's case, 'having a pistol or dag in his hose charged'. Smalbroke successfully sidestepped a swing from Colmore's staff but when he saw Colmore go for his gun he prudently withdrew into his house. Colmore later claimed that he drew the pistol to defend himself against Smalbroke's mastiff. Naturally Smalbroke's instinctive reaction was to seek legal support so he rode over to the nearest JP, Clement Fisher at Packington, to secure a warrant for the arrest of Colmore and Holmes. While there he was warned that suspicious characters were lurking in the lanes and, looking out from a handy upstairs window, he saw Colmore and another companion apparently lying in wait behind a hedge in the lane along which he would ride on his way home. Like the Wise Men in Scripture he returned home 'another way'. The Colmore faction publicly proclaimed their disappointment that Smalbroke had eluded them and that 'nothing but his blood and death should nor could have satisfied them'. What followed was a hilariously confused and ineffective attempt to arrest Thomas Colmore and Thomas Holmes by an obviously unenthusiastic town constable, one Thomas Mychell. It is most entertainingly chronicled by Carl Boardman to whom I am indebted for all the material in this appendix.

Appendix 2:

An Observation on T. W. Hutton's
King Edward's School Birmingham (1552–1952)

It is difficult to be other than sceptical about the following sentence in T. W. Hutton's book:

> It is time now to turn to the men who matter most, [the] Chief Masters (1) ... It is they, in the last resort, who make or mar a school (2); with them one gets the colour of individual personalities (3); with them, finally one gets closest to the life of the schoolboy(4).

Ideas (1) and (2) in the above quotation need some qualifying explanation if they are to be convincing. They make obvious sense in the context of the school's history during its first 300 years. Throughout that period there was daily contact in the classroom between the Chief Master and a fair percentage of the boys, some of whom lived in his house. But as the number of boys in the school increased that percentage decreased and consequently the Chief Master began to recede from the foreground of the lives of an increasing number of boys. The increase in the number of boys entailed an increase in the number of masters (particularly after about 1850) and this, too, diluted the majority of boys' awareness of the Chief Master. However, as his direct influence began to wither away his indirect influence began to grow. He had, of course, always been responsible for the appointment of other masters and this, undoubtedly, had always been a crucially important task; but during the second half of the nineteenth century his wishes and advice were increasingly sought and heeded by the governors, and consequently his influence on general policy, and so on the development of the school, increased. Idea (3) is true enough and it makes Chief Masters a godsend to those writing school histories. Idea (4) is rubbish however you look at it.

Appendix 3:

Expansion in the Eighteenth Century

The governor's meeting of 6 March 1751 is so important and illuminating that it deserves further discussion. The minutes record that:

> [W]e being truly sensible that great numbers of children in this place by reason of the poverty or negligence of their parents are never taught to read the English tongue, and how useful it will be to have many such children taught to read English more than can be taught within the said school, and being earnestly desirous to extend the

said School Charity as far as in us lies for the benefit of the inhabitants of Birmingham, it is therefore ordered by us that four masters or mistresses fit and proper for the teaching of the English language shall forthwith be enquired after and appointed by the said governors ...

Also it is further ordered by us that no master or mistress so to be appointed shall be obliged to have and teach more than forty scholars at one time under the nomination of the said governors which scholars shall likewise continue only during the pleasure of the governors, and that there shall be paid unto each master and mistress so long as he or she hath the full number of forty boys or girls appointed by the said governors the yearly sum of fifteen pounds, but for such time or times as there happens to be a deficiency of that number then to be paid only so much money yearly as shall be in proportion to that sum ...

On 6 November 1751 'the Common Seal was affixed to some Statutes and Orders ... for the appointing of English Schools in different parts within the town of Birmingham'. Six months later still, on 1 April 1752, the approval of the bishop having been obtained, the appointment of the teachers was recorded.

[W]e do nominate and elect William Latham in Dudley Street, Thomas Wilson near the Old Cross, Mary Ankers, wife of Noel Ankers in Freeman Street, and the Widow Austin in London Prentice Street in Birmingham afore said to be the first four masters and mistresses for teaching and instructing such and so many boys and girls to learn the English language as for that purpose be appointed and sent to them from time to time by the said governors.

A few days later on 6 April the schools were advertised in Aris's *Birmingham Gazette*. 'Public Notice' was given that 'such inhabitants of the said town as are esteemed proper objects to have the benefit of the said charity, may forthwith apply to the said governors on the behalf of such children as are intended to be sent to these schools'. The wording of this not exactly gracious advertisement makes it clear that entry to these schools was to be by governors' recommendation – as it had always been for the Grammar School. One wonders just what the criteria were for deciding who were 'proper objects' for the reception of the benefit.

The purpose of these four elementary schools was simply to teach reading and they were intended as an extension of the work of the Petty School where, it may be remembered, only twenty of its pupils were taught writing and arithmetic in addition to reading. It is noticeable that more boys than girls attended the schools where the teacher was a man and more girls than boys where the teacher was a woman. As time passed, however, they seemed gradually to be given over to boys. The Freeman Street school was all male by 1777 and the Old Cross school by 1782, and by 1787 the other two schools were as well. Moreover, by that time the teachers at all four schools were men. Following the institution of these four elementary schools the governors appointed, in 1764, a fifth teacher to teach boys and girls to read in Hockley, explicitly 'for the conveniency of schooling such boys and girls as live in the outer parts of the parish of Birmingham'. Ten years later, in 1774, they established a further elementary school in Shut Lane, and this differed from its predecessors in some imporatant respects. It was, from the outset, intended to be a single-sex purpose-built school with adjacent master's house. The master was to be paid £40 a year – more than was paid to the teachers in the other schools – and he was intended to teach fifty boys writing, drawing and accounts. The concept behind the Shut Lane school makes it clear that the governors saw the necessity for a commercial education in Birmingham.

Index

NOTE: Names in capitals denote Chief Masters (bold type), and Deputy Chief Masters/Second Masters/Ushers (ordinary type). Page numbers in italic indicate illustrations, further reference(s) on the page being in bold italic.